An Analysis of

Frederick Jackson Turner's

The Significance of the Frontier in American History

Joanna Dee Das
with
Joseph Tendler

Published by Macat International Ltd
24:13 Coda Centre, 189 Munster Road, London SW6 6AW.

Distributed exclusively by Routledge
2 Park Square, Milton Park, Abingdon, Oxon OX14 4RN
711 Third Avenue, New York, NY 10017, USA

Routledge is an imprint of the Taylor & Francis Group, an informa business

www.macat.com
info@macat.com

Cataloguing in Publication Data
A catalogue record for this book is available from the British Library.
Library of Congress Cataloguing-in-Publication Data is available upon request.
Cover illustration: Etienne Gilfillan

ISBN 978-1-912302-78-9 (hardback)
ISBN 978-1-912127-86-3 (paperback)
ISBN 978-1-912281-66-4 (e-book)

Notice
The information in this book is designed to orientate readers of the work under analysis,
to elucidate and contextualise its key ideas and themes, and to aid in the development
of critical thinking skills. It is not meant to be used, nor should it be used, as a
substitute for original thinking or in place of original writing or research. References and
notes are provided for informational purposes and their presence does not constitute
endorsement of the information or opinions therein. This book is presented solely for
educational purposes. It is sold on the understanding that the publisher is not engaged
to provide any scholarly advice. The publisher has made every effort to ensure that
this book is accurate and up-to-date, but makes no warranties or representations with
regard to the completeness or reliability of the information it contains. The information
and the opinions provided herein are not guaranteed or warranted to produce particular
results and may not be suitable for students of every ability. The publisher shall not be
liable for any loss, damage or disruption arising from any errors or omissions, or from
the use of this book, including, but not limited to, special, incidental, consequential or
other damages caused, or alleged to have been caused, directly or indirectly, by the
information contained within.

CONTENTS

THE MACAT LIBRARY

The Macat Library is a series of unique academic explorations of seminal works in the humanities and social sciences – books and papers that have had a significant and widely recognised impact on their disciplines. It has been created to serve as much more than just a summary of what lies between the covers of a great book. It illuminates and explores the influences on, ideas of, and impact of that book. Our goal is to offer a learning resource that encourages critical thinking and fosters a better, deeper understanding of important ideas.

Each publication is divided into three Sections: Influences, Ideas, and Impact. Each Section has four Modules. These explore every important facet of the work, and the responses to it.

This Section-Module structure makes a Macat Library book easy to use, but it has another important feature. Because each Macat book is written to the same format, it is possible (and encouraged!) to cross-reference multiple Macat books along the same lines of inquiry or research. This allows the reader to open up interesting interdisciplinary pathways.

To further aid your reading, lists of glossary terms and people mentioned are included at the end of this book (these are indicated by an asterisk [*] throughout) – as well as a list of works cited.

Macat has worked with the University of Cambridge to identify the elements of critical thinking and understand the ways in which six different skills combine to enable effective thinking.
Three allow us to fully understand a problem; three more give us the tools to solve it. Together, these six skills make up the **PACIER** model of critical thinking. They are:

ANALYSIS – understanding how an argument is built
EVALUATION – exploring the strengths and weaknesses of an argument
INTERPRETATION – understanding issues of meaning

CREATIVE THINKING – coming up with new ideas and fresh connections
PROBLEM-SOLVING – producing strong solutions
REASONING – creating strong arguments

To find out more, visit **WWW.MACAT.COM.**

CRITICAL THINKING AND "THE SIGNIFICANCE OF THE FRONTIER IN AMERICAN HISTORY"

Primary critical thinking skill: CREATIVE THINKING
Secondary critical thinking skill: REASONING

Frederick Jackson Turner's 1893 essay on the history of the United States remains one of the most famous and influential works in the American canon.

That is a testament to Turner's powers of creative synthesis; in a few short pages, he succeeded in redefining the way in which whole generations of Americans understood the manner in which their country was shaped, and their own character moulded, by the frontier experience. It is largely thanks to Turner's influence that the idea of America as the home of a sturdily independent people—one prepared, ultimately, to obtain justice for themselves if they could not find it elsewhere—was born. The impact of these ideas can still be felt today: in many Americans' suspicion of "big government," in their attachment to guns—even in *Star Trek's* vision of space as "the final frontier." Turner's thesis may now be criticised as limited (in its exclusion of women) and over-stated (in its focus on the western frontier). That it redefined an issue in a highly impactful way—and that it did so exceptionally eloquently—cannot be doubted.

ABOUT THE AUTHOR OF THE ORIGINAL WORK

Frederick Jackson Turner was born in Portage, Wisconsin in 1861, at the very edge of the American frontier. After completing his PhD at Johns Hopkins University in Baltimore, he returned home as a history professor at the University of Wisconsin. In 1893, Turner unveiled his essay "The Significance of the Frontier in American History" to the American Historical Association, and cemented his reputation as one of the most influential historians in the country. From 1910 to 1924 Turner taught at Harvard University, and he died in 1932 at the age of 70.

ABOUT THE AUTHORS OF THE ANALYSIS

Dr Joanna Dee Das holds a PhD in history from Columbia University. She has taught at Barnard College and Stanford University, and currently teaches at Washington University in St Louis.

Dr Joseph Tendler received his PhD from the University of St Andrews. He is a specialist in historiography, the study of how history is conceived and written, and is the author of *Opponents of the Annales School*.

ABOUT MACAT

GREAT WORKS FOR CRITICAL THINKING

Macat is focused on making the ideas of the world's great thinkers accessible and comprehensible to everybody, everywhere, in ways that promote the development of enhanced critical thinking skills.

It works with leading academics from the world's top universities to produce new analyses that focus on the ideas and the impact of the most influential works ever written across a wide variety of academic disciplines. Each of the works that sit at the heart of its growing library is an enduring example of great thinking. But by setting them in context – and looking at the influences that shaped their authors, as well as the responses they provoked – Macat encourages readers to look at these classics and game-changers with fresh eyes. Readers learn to think, engage and challenge their ideas, rather than simply accepting them.

'Macat offers an amazing first-of-its-kind tool for interdisciplinary learning and research. Its focus on works that transformed their disciplines and its rigorous approach, drawing on the world's leading experts and educational institutions, opens up a world-class education to anyone.'

Andreas Schleicher
Director for Education and Skills, Organisation for Economic Co-operation and Development

'Macat is taking on some of the major challenges in university education … They have drawn together a strong team of active academics who are producing teaching materials that are novel in the breadth of their approach.'

Prof Lord Broers,
former Vice-Chancellor of the University of Cambridge

'The Macat vision is exceptionally exciting. It focuses upon new modes of learning which analyse and explain seminal texts which have profoundly influenced world thinking and so social and economic development. It promotes the kind of critical thinking which is essential for any society and economy.
This is the learning of the future.'

Rt Hon Charles Clarke, former UK Secretary of State for Education

'The Macat analyses provide immediate access to the critical conversation surrounding the books that have shaped their respective discipline, which will make them an invaluable resource to all of those, students and teachers, working in the field.'

Professor William Tronzo, University of California at San Diego

WAYS IN TO THE TEXT

KEY POINTS

- Frederick Jackson Turner (1861–1932) was an American historian whose writing on the American frontier* helped define how we look at history.

- "The Significance of the Frontier" stated that modern America itself originated from European and American experiences of settling in North America.

- The essay combined a new method of studying history with a powerful concept—the frontier—to create a classic in American history that is still relevant over 120 years later.

Who was Frederick Jackson Turner?

Frederick Jackson Turner was born in 1861 and lived at an important time in the development of America. He reshaped how we look at history through his writings on the American frontier (often defined as the line beyond which the open, free land had a population of fewer than two people per square mile). By 1890, Americans had settled all North America, making the geography of the modern USA secure. Yet Turner didn't just study this slice of history: he lived it as well. His hometown of Portage, Wisconsin, once sat on the frontier itself but in Turner's youth it became a settled town. Social and economic developments took place almost daily and this directed

Turner's attention to the life of ordinary Americans from an early age. Turner's father was a journalist and, in political terms, a radical Republican;* his mother was a teacher. Turner himself studied history at the University of Wisconsin and at Johns Hopkins University. In his career as a historian he went a step further than most of his colleagues by persuading politicians to put social reforms in place to improve the lives of Americans. He believed historians could help this process and had a duty to discover the truth about the past, using all available methods. Only in this way, he thought, could progress take place. Turner's timing couldn't have been better—in the early twentieth century calls for social reform were on the increase. And as World War I* approached, so demand grew for intellectuals to explain America's past. As a public intellectual himself, Turner promoted the study of history. He also knew and lobbied many politicians, considering it his duty to bring about positive change.

What Does "The Significance of the Frontier" Say?

What made modern America the way it is? Turner asks this bold question in "The Significance of the Frontier."[1] His answer insists that frontier life shaped the modern American character and its values. In the seventeenth century large numbers of European settlers arrived in America—a land without towns or cities. The Native American* inhabitants roamed the continent, farming to feed their people. In contrast, the first settlers who arrived on the American East Coast built towns that reflected the way they lived in Europe. Then the more adventurous Europeans and their children moved further west in search of farmland and building materials, and so a frontier emerged where settled America met unsettled wilderness. The settlers' experiences taught them determination and also fed a love of individual effort. Yet they also embraced democracy as they learned to live together and confront the difficulties they encountered as a group.

In crafting a precise argument to explain these developments,

Turner used science as a model. He thought historians could write history objectively by looking at sources and extracting facts from them. Such sources should cover a variety of topics, including politics, population, social customs, and trade. By unearthing a range of diverse facts historians would then be able paint a complete picture of what had happened in the past. In this way Turner also became an educational reformer. He pushed historians to practice their trade with the same professionalism as lawyers or businessmen.

Turner's approach broke the mold. Before him, historians had considered America's history as simply an extension of Europe's. However, Turner claimed that the development of America began a new era. This meant that Americans, with their distinctive American ways, held a unique place in the world. As a result, Turner's work gave rise to three new subdisciplines: agricultural history (the story of food supply); environmental history (how the natural world shapes people's lives); and Western history—referring specifically to Western US geography as opposed to the Western world including Europe. This demonstrated the importance of the West at a time when scholars often paid more attention to the East.

Turner made it credible to look at American History in isolation—bringing about a revolution in the way history was studied. He also provided a powerful example for today's American historians by changing the focus of history, as he looked to the mass experience of Americans. Beyond the politics, he asked how everyday life on the frontier shaped American customs and American ideas. It is through Turner that a new approach to history gathered steam in the twentieth century.

Why Does "The Significance of the Frontier" Matter?

You don't have to look far to see the lasting significance of Turner's work. It's not just a matter of how he changed the working methods of historians. He also held a mirror up to America, allowing a nation to see itself clearly for the first time. And his impact remains, reflected in many different fields, from professional scholarship to pop culture.

"The Significance of the Frontier" matters in three ways. First, it supplied a popular version of American identity. Second, it created a new way of writing history. And, third, it developed an idea of the frontier that could be useful in everyday life.

The ideals of intrepid exploring cut to the heart of America's way of life and Turner shows how this relates to the settlement of modern America. His explanation is incomplete on its own, given what we now know, but life on the frontier—cowboys, Indians, and railroads—provides mass entertainment today. And these stories become richer as, for example, knowledge of the African American slave York,* or the Native American Sacajawea,* and their contributions to the history of the frontier filter down to us. They capture the imagination.

Just as a talented journalist might someday make headlines, Turner's work as a historian changed history itself. He organized professional bodies, he encouraged cooperation and he reformed teaching methods. His vision of professional scholarship is now common, while the research-and-development sector, policy analysts, journalists, and businesses all adopted these processes too. Turner's essay shows what focused, professional practice can achieve.

The idea of a frontier is a fertile concept and it appears in many contexts: the "final frontier" of TV's *Star Trek*, for example, owes a debt to Turner. We also see it in the frontiers of knowledge or the frontier between two countries. It evokes exciting images that can range from braving the unknown to transforming a technology or a way of doing things. This makes Turner's work powerful. It shows how history shapes the way we see the world.

"The Significance of the Frontier" is not just a classic history text, it is integral to American history. It explains it, yet is also part of it. What's more, it spotlights the chance to create something new that comes with a new way of life. So the essay forms a touchstone to promote critical thought. It beckons readers to face a problem and push on in search of exciting answers—as did the frontier itself.

NOTES

1   Frederick Jackson Turner, "The Significance of the Frontier in American History," in *The Frontier in American History* (New York: Holt, 1921).

SECTION 1
INFLUENCES

THE AUTHOR AND THE HISTORICAL CONTEXT

KEY POINTS

- "The Significance of the Frontier" remains a key text in American history, both for the frontier* concept it offered and how it founded three new studies: agricultural history, environmental history, and Western history.
- Turner's early life in Portage, Wisconsin, shaped his understanding of the frontier.
- Economic turmoil and social upheaval directed Turner's attention to the lives of everyday Americans.

Why Read this Text?

Readers reap two rewards from Frederick Jackson Turner's "The Significance of the Frontier." First, it offers a classic account of how America came into being. And, second, it provides a glimpse of the way Turner turned his own world as a historian upside down as he paved the way for how historians actually write history today.

Turner argued the now widely recognized position that "American history has been in a large degree the history of the Colonization of the Great West. The existence of an area of free land, its continuous recession, and the advance of American settlement westward, explain American development."[1] But he made sure his arguments didn't only appeal to intellectuals. Turner captured the country's imagination, explaining the emergence of modern America as it tangled with the great wildernesses of pre-US history. In addition, Turner insisted that the historians of America look at regional differences and understand

> ❝ Historical-mindedness is among the most important elements needed in modern civilization. I do not feel that in the past the schools accomplished much in this direction ... history is the 'self-consciousness of humanity.' ❞
>
> Frederick Jackson Turner to American historian Arthur M. Schlesinger, Sr.,* October 22, 1922, in Joseph Tendler, *Opponents of the Annales School*

them. To achieve that, he proposed a strategy. First, they needed to discover many sources of evidence and find different ways of exploring those sources (the methodologies). Second, they had to recognize that historical events had multiple causes. Finally, he challenged historians to show how the past helps to clarify and explain the present. In achieving that, he maintained that history would have popular appeal and a wide use—in politics, business, science, and culture.

Author's Life

Turner was born in Portage, Wisconsin, in 1861 to American-born, professional, white, middle-class parents. His mother taught at a nearby school; his father worked as a journalist and amateur historian.[2] Growing up in Portage, on an authentic American frontier, Turner watched a region in transition. To the east sat sophisticated cities such as New York. In the less-populated West, railroads were beginning to run. As a town that had already been settled, Portage became a place where immigrants, Native Americans* and American-born migrants from the East Coast traded. They also negotiated political agreements and sometimes had violent conflicts that prompted legal and social changes.[3]

Turner's childhood spent watching daily events in Portage helped him develop his ideas. His life provided the best example for him to think about how the frontier defined and shaped American history.

He attended the University of Wisconsin in 1880 and by 1884 had begun his doctoral research at Johns Hopkins University in Baltimore. During his brief time on the East Coast, Turner encountered the dismissive attitudes of many scholars towards his home state and the entire region of the West.[4]

Turner then built a career as an American historian, returning to the University of Wisconsin as a history professor in 1890. In 1910 he moved to Harvard University, where he remained until 1924. In 1922 Turner became visiting scholar to the Huntington Library in Los Angeles, an example of his research activity in libraries and archives across America. Before Turner, historians had failed to undertake such work.[5] He also held a number of important editorial positions. These included working at the *American Historical Review*, America's leading history journal, where he advised on which articles to print and what editorial line to follow.[6]

Author's Background

Turner believed that "each age writes the history of the past anew with reference to the conditions uppermost in its own time."[7] He paid close attention to events of his own lifetime and these are reflected in "The Significance of the Frontier." When he wrote the essay in the summer of 1893 he stressed two issues. First, just three years earlier, the United States Census Bureau had declared the American frontier closed because there was no longer a line beyond which the country was not settled. Second, the previous few months had produced a wave of failing businesses that led to the Panic of 1893*—a huge downturn in the American economy that was to last for over four years.[8]

Turner's ideas met with apathy when he first shared them. He unveiled "The Significance of the Frontier" in a speech before the American Historical Association* in Chicago, but the crowd found a greater thrill in the sights and sounds of the World's Fair. Turner's listeners appeared bored, asked no questions, and his speech turned out to be no match for the debut of the Ferris wheel.[9] Nevertheless Turner engaged with current affairs throughout his career. He kept a close eye on the way modern America emerged from frontier settlement—which is the main thrust of "The Significance of the Frontier."

Within the American university system Turner worked to modernize the way in which history was practiced. At the time he became a professor in 1890, an outgoing generation of older historians were focusing on teaching students to become statesmen and intellectuals: to speak eloquently and write well.[10] This approach responded mainly to the needs of the well-heeled. But Turner insisted that historians should conduct original research and then publish their findings.[11] Before Turner, historians concentrated predominantly on teaching. Their histories were general and their writings were a rehash of past historians' work. They also failed to conduct any significant, original research themselves.[12] It's amazing to consider how lazy that would appear to academics and historians today.

NOTES

1   Frederick Jackson Turner, "The Significance of the Frontier in American History," in *The Frontier in American History* (New York: Holt, 1921), 31.

2   Marnie Hughes-Warrington, "Frederick Jackson Turner (1861–1932)," in *Fifty Key Thinkers on History* (London: Routledge, 2000), 331.

3   Ray Allen Billington, *Frederick Jackson Turner: Historian, Scholar, Teacher* (Oxford: Oxford UP, 1973), 13.

4   Billington, *Frederick Jackson Turner*, 56.

5   Peter Novick, *That Noble Dream: The "Objectivity" Question and the American Historical Profession* (Cambridge: Cambridge UP, 1988), 28.

6   Hughes-Warrington, "Frederick Jackson Turner", 334.

7   Frederick Jackson Turner, "The Significance of History," in *Rereading Frederick Jackson Turner: "The Significance of the Frontier in History" and Other Essays*, ed. John Mack Faragher (New York, NY: Henry Holt, 1991), 18.

8   Martin Ridge, "The Life of an Idea: The Significance of Frederick Jackson Turner's Frontier Thesis," *Montana*: *The Magazine of Western History* 41, no. 1 (1991), 4.

9   Faragher, ed., *Rereading Frederick Jackson Turner*, 1–2.

10   John Higham, *History: Professional Scholarship in America* (Baltimore, MD: Johns Hopkins UP, 1983), 11–13.

11   Allan G. Bogue, "'Not by Bread Alone': The Emergence of the Wisconsin Idea and the Departure of Frederick Jackson Turner," *Wisconsin Magazine of History* 86, no. 1 (2002): 10–23.

12   Higham, *History*, 236–38.

MODULE 2
ACADEMIC CONTEXT

KEY POINTS

- American history sought to explain the origins of modern America.

- "Is America different from the rest of the world?" was the question that dominated American history in Turner's lifetime.

- Turner explained that American history was unique, or "exceptional".

The Work In Its Context

A new way of writing about history emerged in the United States in the nineteenth century and Frederick Jackson Turner's "The Significance of the Frontier" falls squarely in that tradition. Turner (together with fellow American historians such as George Bancroft*) pushed for studying America's rise to world prominence. Until the late nineteenth century, it had been the politics and armies of Great Britain, France, and Russia that had exerted a dominating influence.

Colonizers from European powers had arrived on America's shores since the sixteenth century, founding new ways of life in North America that differed from those of their European backgrounds, yet American historians continued to focus on the histories of the European nations from which they came.[1] Then men such as Turner began to ask important questions. How had modern America begun? And how did it rise to equal or greater importance than the European lands whose people first colonized it? American history was rarely taught until around 1900 and this

> ❝ To the question 'Is America different?' the professional historian is expected to respond with a list of the circumstances and exemptions which have distinguished the history of the United States. ❞
>
> Daniel T. Rodgers, "Exceptionalism"

change only came about because of the work of Turner and men such as his Harvard colleague Edward Channing.*[2]

To write these new histories, Bancroft set the tone for the whole profession by using an approach called positivism,* which uses logic and rationality to discover the truth based on facts compiled from sound evidence.[3] Positivists argued that certain laws govern the growth and development of human society—just like the laws that dictate the physical world. As a consequence, historians should employ evidence-based methods, like scientists, rather than rely on intuition, myth, or stories.

This approach ran counter to the way historians had previously presented history in the manner of a theater play.[4] Charles S. Peirce* and other thinkers of the day vested great importance in science. They recognized how the earliest Americans had sought refuge from political and religious strife and social collapse in a new continent far from Europe.[5]

Overview of the Field

The most important concept in American history throughout Turner's career was exceptionalism.* Simply stated, exceptionalism insists that America differs from the rest of the world, its history revealing a different, better path to that taken by other nations.[6] A typical example of this thinking in historical writing is the notion that God chose America to become the world's leading modern nation in the late nineteenth century. Historian William

A. Dunning* argued that America and Britain stood side-by-side as English-speaking nations, owing to "some special fiat of God."[7] This stood in sharp contrast to nations "elsewhere" that American historians regarded as different, reinforcing their view of America's unique place in the world.[8]

With American exceptionalism came a shift in approach from literary writing based on limited research to rigorous professional history, methodologically conducted. Historians, it was argued, needed to study more than just political, religious, and military history. Widespread support for this idea followed as historians turned their attention to new spheres of interest, including cultural, intellectual, and social history.[9] However, it provoked controversy when historians of these new areas tried to use the methods and concepts of sociology to promote an interdisciplinary method. Sociology worried some American historians because they felt it was imprecise: how could sociologists study something as unwieldy and complicated as society? Renowned academics such as George Burton Adams* supported such questioning, and he wielded influence as president of the American Historical Association.* Adams argued that the growing popularity of sociology resembled "the recrudescence of philosophy."[10] In other words, American historians disliked sociology just as they did philosophy. They dismissed it as a flawed study of knowledge that lacked objectivity.[11]

Academic Influences

Turner worked with William F. Allen* at Wisconsin and Herbert Baxter Adams* at Johns Hopkins in Baltimore,[12] and they encouraged him to explore interdisciplinary history* and research the American West. The similarities between these mentors were crucial; both men had trained as historians in Germany, where they learned to think of history as a science.[13] However, in Germany, "science" simply referred to an organized body of knowledge, whereas, in America, science equaled knowledge gained by laboratory experiments in the life sciences.[14] When Adams and Allen returned to America, they merged German science with its Anglophone cousin. Allen also encouraged Turner to use methods from other subjects to find out more about the past.

Turner rose to the call. In his doctoral studies, he became interested in evolutionary biology* and the way the history of trade revealed key facts about America's past.[15] "The Significance of the Frontier" describes American history as progressing through stages of development, a concept similar to the idea of biological organisms evolving through stages of growth.[16]

The rise of nationalism* also influenced Turner. Nationalism was loyalty, often fierce, to one's nation-state. Scholars and thinkers explained why people should hold allegiance to the national political unit above, say, their home town or even their family. National historians urged scholars to forge "imagined communities" of shared cultural values and common origins.[17] Sharing a single ethnic background often formed the basis for national identity, but the citizens of the United States had many origins. As a nation of immigrants, it required an alternate foundation for American nationalism. In outlining cultural traits that bonded all Americans, Turner's essay provided this foundation—and thus made the nation unique.[18]

NOTES

1   George Brown Tindall and David Emory Shi, *America: A Narrative History* (New York: Norton, 2007), 15–25.

2   Peter Novick, *That Noble Dream: The "Objectivity" Question and the American Historical Profession* (Cambridge: Cambridge UP, 1988), 88.

3   John Higham, *History: Professional Scholarship in America* (Baltimore, MD: Johns Hopkins UP, 1983), 138–9.

4   Novick, *That Noble Dream*, 45.

5   Charles S. Peirce, "How to Make Our Ideas Clear", in *Chance, Love, and Logic*, ed. Morris R. Cohen (New York: Harcourt Brace, 1923), 55–7.

6   Seymour Martin Lipset, *American Exceptionalism: A Double-Edged Sword* (New York: Norton, 1996), 18.

7   William A. Dunning, *The British Empire and the United States: A Review of their Relations During the Century of Peace Following the Treaty of Ghent* (New York: Scribner's Sons, 1914), 357.

8   Daniel T. Rodgers, "Exceptionalism," in *Imagined Histories: American Historians Interpret the Past*, eds. Gordon Wood and Anthony Molho (Princeton, NJ: Princeton UP, 1998), 24.

9   Novick, *That Noble Dream*, 89.

10 Novick, *That Noble Dream*, 91.

11 Fred Morrow Fling, *The Writing of History: An Introduction to Historical Method* (New Haven, CT: Yale UP, 1927), 151.

12 Ray Allen Billington, *Frederick Jackson Turner: Historian, Scholar, Teacher* (Oxford: Oxford UP, 1973), 60.

13 Higham, *History*, 11–12.

14 Fritz K. Ringer, *The Decline of the Mandarins: The German Academic Community, 1890_1933* (Cambridge, MA: Harvard UP, 1969), 102–3, 331–2.

15 Frederick Jackson Turner, *The Character and Influence of the Fur Trade in Wisconsin* (Cambridge, MA: Harvard UP, 1889).

16 Frederick Jackson Turner, "The Significance of the Frontier in American History," in *The Frontier in American History* (New York: Holt, 1921), 3.

17 See Benedict Anderson, *Imagined Communities: Reflections on the Origin and Spread of Nationalism* (London: Verso, 1983), 6.

18 Turner, "The Significance of the Frontier", 1.

MODULE 3
THE PROBLEM

KEY POINTS

- Historians tried to answer two related questions: how could they explain modern American history? And: which methods were most accurate in order to write an objective history?

- On one hand, American history appeared to be a continuation of European history. On the other, it presented a new departure in world history because it was shaped by American frontier life.

- Turner provided the most thorough argument for American history as a new departure—and the culmination of all world history to date.

Core Question

How did the United States of America rise to the mantle of world power? This was at issue in the 1890s when Frederick Jackson Turner wrote "The Significance of the Frontier." This question had two elements. First, which factors helped explain how America had become wealthy and modern? Was it caused by political ideals, economic resources, cultural factors, or something else entirely? And second, underlying this, what methods should Turner and his fellow historians use to discover the answer? In essence, how should they view history? Did it resemble the natural sciences, or was it more similar to well-written, imaginative literature? This second question gained momentum as historians became an important group among a new generation of professional university teachers.[1] In the early nineteenth century, university professors had supported themselves

> ** ❝ While respecting America's indebtedness and affiliation to Europe, the leading historians assumed that liberty was distinctively the essence of American nationality. ❞**
>
> John Higham, *History: Professional Scholarship in America*

as private individuals, enthusiastically collecting information about the past. But the new breed wanted to behave like a formal group of professionals—just as lawyers or business leaders did—with their own organizations and agreed conventions.[2]

The Participants

As historians pondered their methods and models, answers came from different groups and individuals. John Franklin Jameson* exhaustively promoted the cause of professional unity as he helped organize the American Historical Association* and its journal, the *American Historical Review*.[3] He also supported those who sought to expand American history in the university curriculum so that it might someday eclipse European history. Alongside Jameson, a generation of older historians, including George Burton Adams* and Herbert Baxter Adams,* also responded. They supported both the "what to do" (how to discover the truth about America's past) and the "how to do it" (how to organize historians and research institutions to complete the task successfully).[4]

Men of Turner's age followed. Edward Channing,* for example, sought to popularize the teaching and publication of American history even though in his early years he had struggled to secure a job in that field; in 1880, Harvard's president told him: "Your desire to teach American history is a laudable one, but you of course recognize the practical necessity of having other strings to your bow."[5] Albert Bushnell Hart,* also of Channing's generation, pursued the same course, which went hand in hand with efforts to separate American history from European history. Now that America was a world force to reckon with, the time was ripe to make its history a subject in its own right.

The Contemporary Debate

Turner adopted the ideas of the older generation but he also challenged them. He believed a scientific approach was part of the professional practice of history as a university professor,[6] but he rejected the connection between Europe and America drawn by Herbert Baxter Adams. Adams argued that a similarity existed between village formation and social trends in medieval Germany and early-modern America; he called this germ theory,* drawing from the study of the way diseases spread (he saw social growth patterns as an extension of the theory that germs, or bacteria, spread illness between people).[7] Likewise, William Dunning* sought to show that Britain and America had long-term strategic links stretching far back into the past.[8]

George Bancroft* and Edward Channing offered an alternative explanation. They regarded American history less as an outgrowth of Europe's past than as a unique series of events and factors[9] culminating in the formation of the United States as a result of the American Civil War.* So, in the three centuries since colonization, these historians of the late-nineteenth and early-twentieth centuries saw a new phase in world history that was totally different from European history.[10] This began the long strand of American exceptionalism,* an idea that is still current today. Owing to "a political culture which has pinned so many of its ideals to faith in its own uniqueness," [11] America has forged a role that sets it apart from all other nations—even its near neighbors.

NOTES

1   John Higham, *History: Professional Scholarship in America* (Baltimore, MD: Johns Hopkins UP, 1983), 265.

2   Peter Novick, *That Noble Dream: The "Objectivity" Question and the American Historical Profession* (Cambridge: Cambridge UP, 1988), 48–9.

3   Arthur E. Bestor Jr., "The Transformation of American Scholarship, 1875–1917," *The Library Quarterly* 23, no. 3 (1953): 175.

4   Thomas L. Haskell, *The Emergence of Professional Social Science: The American Social Science Association and the Nineteenth-Century Crisis of Authority* (Baltimore, MD: Johns Hopkins UP, 1977), 172.

5   Eliot to Channing, June 23, 1880, in Joseph Tendler, *Opponents of the Annales School* (Basingstoke: Palgrave, 2013), 159.

6   Frederick Jackson Turner, "The Significance of History," in *Rereading Frederick Jackson Turner: "The Significance of the Frontier in History" and Other Essays*, ed. John Mack Faragher (New York, NY: Henry Holt, 1991), 23–4.

7   Herbert Baxter Adams, *The Germanic Origin of New England Towns* (Baltimore, MD: Johns Hopkins UP, 1882).

8   William A. Dunning, *The British Empire and the United States: A Review of their Relations During the Century of Peace Following the Treaty of Ghent* (New York: Scribner's Sons, 1914).

9   George Bancroft, *History of the United States from the Discovery of the American Continent* (6 vols.; Boston, MA: Little and Brown, 1834); Edward Channing, *A History of the United States* (6 vols.; New York: Macmillan, 1905–25).

10 Bancroft, *History of the United States*, vol. 6, iv–vii; Channing, *A History of the United States*, vol. 6, 13–18.

11 Daniel T. Rodgers, "Exceptionalism," in *Imagined Histories: American Historians Interpret the Past*, eds. Gordon Wood and Anthony Molho (Princeton, NJ: Princeton UP, 1998), 35.

MODULE 4
THE AUTHOR'S CONTRIBUTION

KEY POINTS

- Turner argued that, on the frontier,* encounters with the wilderness and Native Americans* formed a unique American spirit of endeavor, along with a love of freedom and democracy.

- The frontier thesis provided the most compelling examination of the modern American character by using a scientific method applied to a variety of causes and events.

- Turner departed entirely from preceding interpretations of American history.

Author's Aims

Frederick Jackson Turner claimed only modest aims in "The Significance of the Frontier," however his intentions were bold and twofold. First, he called for a more analytical approach to history. Narrative history told stories; analysis provided the how and why that explained change over time. Rather than just recite facts, historians needed to make arguments and give broad interpretations.[1] In abandoning simple chronological history or in-depth biographical detail of leaders, Turner broke new ground. In fewer than 30 pages, he crafted a sweeping explanation of how and why societies on the North American continent had changed over the course of 250 years. He likened his essay to reading American social evolution itself: "Line by line as we read this continental page from West to East we find the record of social evolution."[2] In this way Turner challenged the older generation of American historians. Not only did he explain American history in scientific terms, but he also focused on new subfields, such as geographical and social history.[3]

> 66 The American frontier is sharply distinguished from the European frontier—a fortified boundary line running through dense populations. The most significant thing about the American frontier is that it lies at the hither edge of free land. In the census reports it is treated as the margin of that settlement which has a density of two or more to the square mile. The term is an elastic one, and for our purposes does not need sharp definition. We shall consider the whole frontier belt, including the Indian country and the outer margin of the 'settled area' of the census reports. This paper will make no attempt to treat the subject exhaustively; its aim is simply to call attention to the frontier as a fertile field for investigation, and to suggest some of the problems which arise in connection with it. 99
>
> Frederick Jackson Turner, "The Significance of the Frontier"

Second, Turner shifted the focus of American history away from Europe and the East Coast to the West, and explained American history through developments unique to the United States. In so doing he reacted strongly against the older generation of historians as represented by Herbert Baxter Adams* and his germ theory.* In making the break, Turner provided the strongest exceptionalist* explanation up to that time.[4]

Turner also intended his text to respond to current events. The essay begins: "In a recent bulletin of the Superintendent of the Census for 1890 appear these significant words: 'Up to and including 1880 the country had a frontier of settlement, but at present the unsettled area has been so broken into by isolated bodies of settlement that there can hardly be said to be a frontier line. In the discussion of its extent, its westward movement, etc., it can not, therefore, any longer have a place in the census reports.'"[5]

Turner therefore was trying to clarify the "first period" of American history.[6] If the frontier had vanished because America had been settled, then the American constitution, along with the political and social institutions it had produced, would grow and change. Turner intended to show that what made Americans American was the effect of the frontier, a factor that made America's experience exceptional and provided a new opportunity for the world.[7]

Approach

Turner approached his argument, known as "the frontier thesis," using both an analytical narrative and the positivist* method of mining documents for facts to insert into a single chronology (both methods were widespread in America in the 1890s). He arrived at this key concept by combining his childhood experiences in Portage, Wisconsin, with his scholarly training at the University of Wisconsin and Johns Hopkins University. As a child on the Wisconsin frontier, Turner witnessed the forging of an industrious, independent, and pragmatic frontier spirit. In Portage, immigrants from several different countries mingled with migrants from the East Coast and Native Americans. Together they traded and built a thriving economy fueled by free land and unfettered agriculture.[8]

Besides drawing on his childhood experiences, Turner followed his mentors and adopted the intellectual framework of positivism* as a means of understanding Portage.[9] He delved into the work of historians such as George Bancroft* and conducted his own research on frontier town life. This enabled him to tell the story of the frontier and how it had evolved since the eighteenth century. Bancroft's literary elegance is not lost on Turner, whose chronological survey of the frontier has its own style. Without citing any evidence, Turner insists that "from the time the mountains rose between the pioneer and the seaboard, a new order of Americanism arose." He adds: "The West and the East began to get out of touch of each other. The settlements from the sea to the mountains kept connection with the rear and had a certain solidarity."[10]

Contribution In Context

Turner's work proved highly innovative in its own time and beyond. The essay was as sweeping as the American vista itself. He tackled the stages of frontier development; interactions with Native Americans; slavery; the question of democracy; and other major points. Yet these were secondary to Turner's main premise. He insisted that United States history up to 1890 was primarily one of ordinary people engaged in westward expansion—and not the haughty chronicles of presidents or politicians such as those written by Herbert Baxter Adams* and Bancroft.

This premise produced a fundamental change of approach in the study of American history. It didn't take place right away, but by the 1900s, and certainly by 1920, it had transformed American history from a story of continuous development rooted in European civilization into a multiple-causes process focused on the frontier.[11]

NOTES

1   Frederick Jackson Turner, "The Significance of the Frontier in American History," in *The Frontier in American History* (New York: Holt, 1921), 18.

2   Turner, "The Significance of the Frontier," 11.

3   Peter Novick, *That Noble Dream: The "Objectivity" Question and the American Historical Profession* (Cambridge: Cambridge UP, 1988), 33.

4   Daniel T. Rodgers, "Exceptionalism," in *Imagined Histories: American Historians Interpret the Past*, eds. Gordon Wood and Anthony Molho (Princeton, NJ: Princeton UP, 1998), 24–6.

5   Turner, "The Significance of the Frontier," 1.

6   Turner, "The Significance of the Frontier," 38.

7   John Mack Faragher, ed., *Rereading Frederick Jackson Turner: "The Significance of the Frontier in History" and Other Essays* (New York, NY: Henry Holt, 1991), 8.

8   Ray Allen Billington, *Frederick Jackson Turner: Historian, Scholar, Teacher* (Oxford: Oxford UP, 1973), 13–14.

9   John Higham, *History: Professional Scholarship in America* (Baltimore, MD: Johns Hopkins UP, 1983), 174–5.

10 Turner, "The Significance of the Frontier," 18.

11 Rodgers, "Exceptionalism," 26.

SECTION 2
IDEAS

MODULE 5
MAIN IDEAS

KEY POINTS

- The book's key themes are: free land encourages people to develop democratic and freedom-loving ideals; geography determines human society as much as humans do; and the social and political formation of the American nation.

- "The Significance of the Frontier" argues that the movement of American settlers towards the West created a geographical, social, and economic process that created a nation.

- Turner presented this argument as a concise essay without in-depth analysis of data, designed to reach a popular audience.

Key Themes

Three key themes run throughout Frederick Jackson Turner's "The Significance of the Frontier." First, deserted wilderness land presented unique opportunities both for farming and freedom.[1] Such freedoms did not exist in settled towns or villages. Untamed nature challenged settlers to respond creatively to their environment as they struggled for survival and, as a consequence, wilderness helped form America. This idea chimed with a general perception in the nineteenth century inherited from the first settlers who revered uninhabited areas of wilderness, free from the constraints of social customs. At the time of Turner's writing American politicians set up schemes to preserve wilderness areas, now known as the national parks, to protect areas of untamed nature in North America as a reminder of the country's origins.[2]

❝ In the case of the United States we have a different phenomenon. Limiting our attention to the Atlantic coast, we have the familiar phenomenon of the evolution of institutions in a limited area, such as the rise of representative government; the differentiation of simple colonial governments into complex organs; the progress from primitive industrial society, without division of labor, up to manufacturing civilization. But we have in addition to this a recurrence of the process of evolution in each western area reached in the process of expansion. **❞**

Frederick Jackson Turner, "The Significance of the Frontier"

Second, Turner argues that geography plays a key role in human behavior and that "social development" goes hand in hand with the areas where societies exist.[3] Third, and finally, Turner analyzes the idea of a "nation." He asks: what makes up a nation state? Is it simply geographical unity? Or does it have interstate coherence? Probing deeper, Turner inquires how American institutions such as the constitution, democracy, and the rule of law have emerged.[4]

Exploring The Ideas

Turner argued that the border between America's settled East and unexplored West spawned and shaped American ways of life. Since the arrival of the Pilgrim Fathers* in 1620, the European behavior and social customs of Americans had been challenged by the unknown wilderness they found on the frontier.*[5] Society evolved in stages as colonizing Europeans encountered indigenous populations and uninhabited areas. First, the Europeans began to trade with the hunter-gatherer Native Americans.* Then, the settlers developed farming—initially at a subsistence level simply to feed themselves and later as commercial agriculture. Finally, settlements grew into industrialized, urbanized areas.[6] The frontier line then moved further West and the process repeated itself, except that the "'civilized" part became less tied to its European ancestry. And so each successive wave of the frontier created an increasingly "American" character.[7]

The overall result of this process, Turner insisted, was an Americanization of European settlers and their descendants. "The result is that to the frontier the American intellect owes its striking characteristics. That coarseness and strength combined with acuteness and inquisitiveness; that practical, inventive turn of mind, quick to find expedients; that masterful grasp of material things, lacking in the artistic but powerful to effect great ends; that restless, nervous energy; that dominant individualism, working for good and for evil, and withal that buoyancy and exuberance which comes with freedom—these are traits of the frontier, or traits called out elsewhere because of the existence of the frontier."[8]

Each time the frontier moved westward in the nineteenth century—until it reached the Pacific Coast—the people behind it became progressively more American. Individualism and democracy became buzzwords that described citizens of a society in dramatic transformation. In Turner's view, these qualities gave modern Americans their resilience to build a free society.[9]

Encounters with the frontier also shaped modern American politics. Turner argued that with each successive wave of frontier expansion, similar political questions arose. How would settlers administer and distribute the newly acquired public lands? And how would they interact with the native population already living in those lands?[10] As the frontier shifted, the constant need for people to renegotiate these questions helped forge a unique American character.[11]

This point of view challenged American history as historians had previously understood it. For example, Turner rejected the idea that American institutions inherited anything particular from

Europe. This opinion went against the views of American historian William Dunning,* who backed the notion that America had a close connection to Britain, in part because of their shared language. Turner also challenged a Western history built on romanticized stories of cowboys and vigilante justice.[12] Turner's frontier thesis gave the history of the American West a key role in the formation of America itself.

The question of nationality also came in for Turner's scrutiny. First, he argued that, as frontier peoples of various nationalities interacted, they created a "composite nationality."[13] That concept parallels the notion of America as a melting pot.

Second, the frontier created a sense of national identity. It demanded national responses to matters such as taxes, the administration and distribution of public lands, and the development of roads and bridges.[14] Turner insisted that the slavery question was less important than the broader national economic questions that the frontier posed.[15] The slavery question arose in the first half of the nineteenth century, from around 1800 until the end of the American Civil War* and the abolition of slavery in 1865. It asked whether Americans should outlaw slavery because it was, among other things, inhumane. The American Civil War itself began in part as a conflict between Abolitionists, who wanted to outlaw slavery, and those in the Southern slave-owning states who did not.[16] Turner thought that, in the broader context of American history as understood through the frontier, the slavery question became insignificant: "when American history comes to be rightly viewed it will be seen that the slavery question is an incident."[17]

Third, the frontier promoted the development of democracy.[18] Yet Turner also sounded a word of warning—individualism bred on the frontier had its good and bad sides. He noted in particular that it could create anti-social behavior and hostility to political and lawful control.[19]

Language And Expression

Turner's arguments are easily followed. He presented his ideas in clear and persuasive prose —though not always in the most enlightened language for twenty-first century readers. For example, his use of the word "savage" to describe Native Americans serves as a reminder that nineteenth-century beliefs in the hierarchy of civilizations and the biological inferiority of certain races shapes Turner's thesis. This requires contemporary readers to modify his arguments to grasp their present-day relevance.

The rhetorical elements in his writing speak to Turner's engagement in American political life. He chose to address the American Historical Association* about the frontier in 1893 because by then that frontier had closed. Since Turner thought the frontier was the driving force in American history to that point in time, he claimed that its closure left Americans facing an uncertain future in which they would have to abandon their frontier mentality and find a new way of defining themselves.[20]

NOTES

1   Frederick Jackson Turner, "The Significance of the Frontier in American History," in *The Frontier in American History* (New York: Holt, 1921), 22.

2   Robert M. Utley, "Yellowstone and the National Park Concept, 1872–1972," in *Western American History in the Seventies: Selected Papers Presented to the First Western History Conference, Colorado State University, August 10–12, 1972*, ed. Daniel Tyler (Fort Collins, CO: Robinson for Educational Media & Information Systems, 1972), 7–13.

3   Turner, "The Significance of the Frontier," 3.

4   Turner, "The Significance of the Frontier," 2.

5   Turner, "The Significance of the Frontier," 37.

6   Turner, "The Significance of the Frontier," 31.

7   Turner, "The Significance of the Frontier," 12.

8   Turner, "The Significance of the Frontier," 37.

9   Turner, "The Significance of the Frontier," 38.

10 Turner, "The Significance of the Frontier," 15–16.

11 Turner, "The Significance of the Frontier," 18.

12 James R. Grossman, "Introduction," in *The Frontier in American Culture: An Exhibition at the Newberry Library, August 26, 1994–January 7, 1995* (Berkeley, CA: California UP, 1994), 1.

13 Turner, "The Significance of the Frontier," 22, 28.

14 Turner, "The Significance of the Frontier," 30.

15 Turner, "The Significance of the Frontier," 3.

16 George Brown Tindall and David Emory Shi, *America: A Narrative History* (New York: Norton, 2007), 390–1.

17 Turner, "The Significance of the Frontier," 24.

18 Turner, "The Significance of the Frontier," 30.

19 Turner, "The Significance of the Frontier," 30–1.

20 Turner, "The Significance of the Frontier," 38.

MODULE 6
SECONDARY IDEAS

KEY POINTS

- One of the main secondary ideas in *Bowling Alone* is the distinction between bridging* and bonding* social capital.*

- "The Significance of the Frontier" also considers what makes up American nationalism* and urges historians to practice scientific and interdisciplinary history*—and to put history at the service of American political culture.

- These secondary ideas relate closely to Turner's main ideas and also show his commitment to social reform and political activism.

- The concept that history is useful to American political culture forms Turner's most important secondary idea.

Other Ideas

In "The Significance of the Frontier," Frederick Jackson Turner considers how the American frontier* shaped a unique history unlike any found in a European nation. But he also puts forward two crucial secondary ideas that are easy to miss in a short essay.

First, Turner argues that the frontier gave birth to American nationalism.[1] Here he talks not so much about the nation's formation but of the national imagination: how Americans themselves saw their country in contrast to other nations. Second, Turner promotes a new concept of history's place in public life—namely, that the historical is also the political.

Turner proposed a history that engaged in present politics rather than isolating itself inside universities and academia. Turner saw

> ** And now, four centuries from the discovery of
> America, at the end of a hundred years of life under
> the Constitution, the frontier has gone, and with its
> going has closed the first period of American history. **
> Frederick Jackson Turner, "The Significance of the Frontier"

late-nineteenth- and twentieth-century America beginning a new
phase of development as a settled nation—one that posed dangers
because the closure of the frontier marked a break with America's
past. Seeing the closure as a rupture, rather than a continuation,
put Turner at odds with an older, more conservative generation
of historians. Herbert Baxter Adams* and George Bancroft* not
only ignored the frontier's role, but also saw modern America as an
accumulation of its entire past.[2]

Exploring The Ideas

Turner relied on three ideas in arguing that the frontier forged
American nationalism. First, he stated that because Americans needed
to trade and negotiate with Native Americans,* they had come to see
themselves in contrast to the indigenous peoples they encountered.[3]
As they advanced westward into the frontier, the colonists needed
common measures of defense against (and systems of engagement
with) Native Americans. Indeed, "the trading frontier, while steadily
undermining Indian power by making the tribes ultimately dependent
on the whites, yet, through its sale of guns, gave to the Indian increased
power of resistance to the farming frontier."[4] Turner also cited the
Congress of Albany of 1754* as an example of an early nationalist
political agreement that was borne out of the need to establish laws
and regulations governing interactions with Native Americans.

Second, he insisted that slavery was not the defining issue of the
United States prior to 1861. Instead, questions of trade, selling of

public lands, and other economic concerns took precedence. Dealing with these questions forged national unity: that is, nationalism based on an imagined and self-defined American democracy.[5]

Third, he proposed that the frontier was an extension of the Middle Atlantic* region of the United States. It boasted more ethnic, religious, economic, and social diversity than Puritan* New England or Southern plantations where slaves were used to farm tobacco, sugar, and cotton. Thus, it was more open to creating a cosmopolitan nationalism similar to the society fostered in Turner's own lifetime.[6]

A call for a new kind of history also informs "The Significance of the Frontier." Turner ends on an optimistic note: "Since the days when the fleet of Columbus sailed into the waters of the New World, America has been another name for opportunity, and the people of the United States have taken their tone from the incessant expansion which has not only been open but has even been forced upon them."[7]

Turner here gives voice to views he expressed elsewhere. With the frontier closed, American "opportunity" and American "democracy" needed to undergo reform to ensure their survival in the modern world. The values of frontier settlements—individualism, freedom, trade, and the promotion of prosperity—counted on necessary reforms to survive. By making this point about reform, Turner encourages American politicians to consider the needs and hopes of American society.[8] But he did not overplay this in his histories. Instead, he saved full expressions of his political views for private conversations and pamphlets on social reform.[9]

Overlooked

Because "The Significance of the Frontier" has become a classic, few areas of its argument have gone unnoticed in the last 120 years.[10] Yet, because the frontier represents just one aspect of his analysis of American history, scholars have neglected Turner's broader thesis. His essay on the frontier depicted "the West" as a constantly moving boundary line that shifted each time social development occurred.[11] Thus the West was not static but active, always transforming from wild frontier to settled communities. This led Turner in a number of directions in his work on social history, but those explorations have failed to attract as much attention as his frontier thesis.[12]

In condemning Turner for racism and American exceptionalism,* historians have nevertheless overlooked progressive and even radical aspects of his frontier thesis. Take, for example, his idea of a "mixed race" American identity. This challenged the existing idea that America was fundamentally an Anglo-Saxon* nation. What's more, his notion of a secular, non-religious, American character offered space for non-Christians to feel a part of the nation. He also warns about the dangers of excessive individualism on the frontier. This challenges the interpretation of his thesis as completely positive and pro-American. Though his essay reinforced nationalistic ideas, at least those ideas were more inclusive in their thinking about the nation's community than previous nationalist histories.[13]

NOTES

1 Jörg Nagler, "From Culture to *Kultur*: American Perceptions of Imperial Germany, 1871–1914," in *Transatlantic Images and Perceptions: Germany and America Since 1776*, eds. David E. Barclay and Elisabeth Glaser-Schmidt (Cambridge: Cambridge UP, 1997), 143.

2 Peter Novick, *That Noble Dream: The "Objectivity" Question and the American Historical Profession* (Cambridge: Cambridge UP, 1988), 93.

3 Frederick Jackson Turner, "The Significance of the Frontier in American History," in *The Frontier in American History* (New York: Holt, 1921), 13–14.

4 Turner, "The Significance of the Frontier," 13.

5 Turner, "The Significance of the Frontier," 24.

6 Turner, "The Significance of the Frontier," 27.

7 Turner, "The Significance of the Frontier," 37.

8   Novick, *That Noble Dream*, 93

9   Frederick Jackson Turner, "Social Forces in American History," *American Historical Review* 16, no. 2 (1911): 319, 321.

10 Daniel T. Rodgers, "Exceptionalism," in *Imagined Histories: American Historians Interpret the Past*, eds. Gordon Wood and Anthony Molho (Princeton, NJ: Princeton UP, 1998), 25.

11 Turner, "The Significance of the Frontier," 6.

12 Frederick Jackson Turner, *The Significance of Sections in American History*, ed. Max Farrand (New York, NY: Henry Holt, 1932).

13 Ray Allen Billington, *The Genesis of the Frontier Thesis: A Study in Historical Creativity* (San Marino, CA: Huntington Library, 1971), 42.

MODULE 7
ACHIEVEMENT

KEY POINTS

- Turner succeeded in explaining the origin of modern America.

- Americans hungry for professional historians to explain the nation's past enhanced the success of "The Significance of the Frontier."

- Nineteenth-century beliefs in social and ethnic hierarchies limited the success that "The Significance of the Frontier" could have enjoyed subsequently.

Assessing The Argument

In only 38 pages, Frederick Jackson Turner's "The Significance of the Frontier" achieves his three aims. First, he examines the frontier* as an arena where American identity is created and acted out. Second, he writes a history engaged in the current affairs of 1890s America. Third, he proposes a new kind of historical writing that stands in sharp contrast to the conservative, Europe-leaning works of an older generation.

The work did not make an immediate impact, in that his audience barely reacted when he unveiled "The Significance of the Frontier" as a speech in 1893. However, Turner's history engaged with the public on current affairs, and with his professional peers as a breaker of the mold in history writing. By 1920, when the text formed the first essay in a collection entitled *The Frontier in American History*, historians greeted it as authored "by one of the best loved members in the guild of American historians."[1] Reviewers also suspected that "there is probably not a student or a teacher of American history anywhere who will not in time come under the influence of this book."[2]

> 66 Turner deflected the trend of American historiography [the writing of history] from its old channel into a new course where it is inseparable from the whole body of economics, sociology, and geography, as well as history. 99
>
> Frederic L. Paxson, review of *The Significance of Sections in American History*

Achievement In Context

The changing of the guard among historians and the drive of American universities to become more professional helped popularize Turner's frontier thesis. Turner's insistence that "American social development has been continually beginning over again on the frontier"[3] introduced a new concept of instability into American history. If American society had remade itself over and over again on the frontier, then it had not expanded in a stable fashion—as Herbert Baxter Adams* and an older generation of historians insisted it should be taught. American history, they asserted, should be "taken as an advanced subject, with the purpose of getting a clear idea of the course of events in the building of the American Republic and the development of its political ideas."[4]

But if American history continually changed due to forces on the frontier—from trade to cooperation with Native Americans*— then Baxter and his fellows had it all wrong. Turner urged that his colleagues look at a range of causes of events, using not only science but sociology and other new disciplines.[5]

In addition, the emergence of a climate for reform in American culture drew strength from Turner's arguments. This ran in parallel with the desire of Turner and others to promote a professional approach in the study of history. Historians, economists, and social scientists (among them Turner's friend, the political scientist and future US President, Woodrow Wilson*) wanted to examine how culture, society, and politics evolved in its historical context.[6] As a result, the old view that stable structures such as European institutions were the foundation of American life collapsed. Now scholars examined the singular nature of events. Their ultimate purpose was to agree on the means to preserve the best in American democracy and society and, where necessary, suggest paths to reform and improvement.[7]

Limitations

At first glance, "The Significance of the Frontier" may seem limited by its late-nineteenth-century cultural context. Yet in some ways Turner meant the essay to have such limitations. He believed that even though historians studied the past, they should always write with an eye on the present. True to this belief, he focused on regions within the United States in the twentieth century because he believed the closing of the frontier required examination of the history of regional interaction.[8]

That said, some attitudes that Turner expresses in "The Significance of the Frontier" are out of place today and are no longer recognized by scholars as they are tainted by outmoded opinions commonplace 120 years ago. These include elements of racism and a belief that inequality between ethnic groups is biologically determined.

The American context of the frontier thesis, however, doesn't form an impediment for contemporary readers, as might at first be thought. Indeed, twentieth-century scholars went on to study frontiers throughout the past and across the globe. One high point of this trend came with a symposium at the University of Wisconsin, where Turner once worked. The essays that resulted would have made him proud. In this collection, frontiers became subjects of study in the Roman colonization of Europe at the beginning of European civilization and in the movement westward of the Russian frontier into Europe.[9] The movement of the Russian border sparked particular interest in the mid-twentieth century as Cold War* tensions grew between America and Europe on one side, and communist Russia on the other. In this way, Turner's notion of a frontier found global applications.

NOTES

1   Edmond S. Meany, "Review of Frederick Jackson Turner, *The Frontier in American History*," *The Washington Historical Quarterly* 12, no. 1 (1921): 73.

2   Meany, "Review of Turner, *The Frontier in American History*," 73.

3   Frederick Jackson Turner, "The Significance of the Frontier in American History," in *The Frontier in American History* (New York: Holt, 1921), 2.

4   Herbert Baxter Adams et al., *The Study of History in Schools* (New York: Macmillan, 1899), 74.

5   Frederick Jackson Turner, "The Significance of History," in *Rereading Frederick Jackson Turner: "The Significance of the Frontier in History" and Other Essays*, ed. John Mack Faragher (New York, NY: Henry Holt, 1991), 14.

6   Thomas L. Haskell, *The Emergence of Professional Social Science: The American Social Science Association and the Nineteenth-Century Crisis of Authority* (Baltimore, MD: Johns Hopkins UP, 1977), 33–45.

7   Frederick Jackson Turner, "Social Forces in American History," *American Historical Review* 16, no. 2 (1911): 120.

8   Michael Steiner, "From Frontier to Region: Frederick Jackson Turner and the New Western History," *Pacific Historical Review* 64, no. 4 (1995): 479–501.

9   Walker D. Wyman and Clifton D. Kroeber, *The Frontier in Perspective* (Madison, WI: Wisconsin UP, 1957).

MODULE 8
PLACE IN THE AUTHOR'S WORK

KEY POINTS

- Turner's life work explored the social and geographical origins of modern America.

- "The Significance of the Frontier" made Turner's reputation and began a research agenda that he worked on until he died.

- Turner's frontier thesis is his most important work.

Positioning

Frederick Jackson Turner's "The Significance of the Frontier" remained his most important work, central to the research he went on to undertake. Though written only four years after he began his career as a professor, it condensed many years of thought and research.[1] "The Significance of the Frontier" also remained Turner's most important work because, for the rest of his career, Turner chose not to produce any extended pieces of writing. Instead, he continued to research and write on American history in essay format. Meanwhile, "The Significance of the Frontier" gained further attention as it was republished as part of an essay collection in 1920.[2]

Turner's later work focused on the history and interaction of America's regions in creating American national politics. His collection of essays, *The Significance of Sections in American History,* won the Pulitzer Prize for History in 1932. This work further extended the social history that received only brief attention in Turner's frontier thesis.[3]

University of Wisconsin Professor William Cronon,* himself inspired by Turner's frontier thesis, argued that Turner's earlier essay, "The

> 66 Turner's was not the task of producing narrative history; it was something far more important. It was to go behind events and to seek the whys and hows of things and thereby furnish hints of meanings to a generation of more plodding historians. 99
>
> Avery Craven, "Frederick Jackson Turner, Historian"

Significance of History," would have been groundbreaking had it been written by a professor at a major East Coast university and published in a notable journal.[4] Instead, Turner was a young professor at the University of Wisconsin and published the essay in the little-read *Wisconsin Journal of Education.* As a result, scholars did not find out about it for decades.

In the essay, Turner laid out several arguments championing the study of social history and "ordinary" people, whereas historians of his generation typically studied the political exploits of kings and presidents. He also called on historians to use a variety of sources in their work, borrowing from religion, psychology, or any other field that could help explain the analytical problems presented by the study of history. Today the popularity of global history and interdisciplinary study attests to the forward-thinking nature of his approach. So does his open-mindedness to new methods: "history, both objective and subjective, is ever *becoming*, never completed."[5]

After the success of "The Significance of the Frontier in American History," Turner turned to a study of "sections." Once an area was settled, it turned from a frontier into a section—a community that developed its own habits and structures. Turner examined the relationships between America's sections in *The Significance of Sections in American History*, published after his death.[6] His thesis about sections, however, was never influential outside academic circles.[7] Instead, his frontier thesis continued to dominate the general public's understanding of American history.

Integration

Turner's focus on, and devotion to, American history meant that "The Significance of the Frontier" and his later work all stemmed from a common source and as a result his overall output is coherent. His deep involvement with American current affairs, albeit from a distance, and belief in putting history at the service of the general population, also meant that his work had an impact on American intellectual life. In the first years of World War I,* with America divided over whether or not to enter the conflict, Turner's view that America should stay out of the war for as long as possible influenced many, including his personal friend President Woodrow Wilson.*[8]

Because of this, it is important to see "The Significance of the Frontier" within Turner's overall output. It is not just an essay about the settlement of America, or the future identity of the United States. Instead, Turner demonstrates his commitment to the history of ordinary Americans, the lower classes who propped up the settlement towns on the frontier in the nineteenth century, along with the working population across America's sections whose hopes and aspirations played themselves out in presidential and congressional elections into the twentieth century.[9] For this reason, Turner must be seen as part of a wider social and cultural debate within America that continues today.[10]

Significance

Turner's "The Significance of the Frontier" remains without doubt his most influential work. At the end of the twentieth century the last detailed review of its impact observed, "Turner's essay is the single most influential piece of writing in the history of American history."[11] Such a bold claim is not isolated. Prominent American historians such as William Appleman Willams* had earlier reported that Turner's "thesis rolled through universities and into popular literature as a tidal wave."[12] Yet, beneath this level of national fame,

Turner's work did not give rise to a particular school of thought or historical method. Instead, his activities prompted different streams of development. On the one hand, his social history and political reformism played into the New History* of the twentieth century, which studied social inequality so as to show the need for and suggest political and social reform.[13] On the other hand, Turner's tireless activities—lecturing school history teachers and promoting institutions and professional organizations that supported history teaching and research—raised the profile of his interdisciplinary and open-minded approach to the past.[14]

NOTES

1 Ray Allen Billington, *Frederick Jackson Turner: Historian, Scholar, Teacher* (Oxford: Oxford UP, 1973), 128.

2 Frederick Jackson Turner, *The Frontier in American History* (New York, NY: Henry Holt, 1920), 1–38.

3 Edmond S. Meany, "Review of Frederick Jackson Turner *The Significance of Sections in American History*," *Washington Historical Quarterly* 24, no. 4 (1933): 304.

4 William Cronon, "Revisiting the Vanishing Frontier: The Legacy of Frederick Jackson Turner," *Western Historical Quarterly* 18, no. 2 (1987): 161.

5 Frederick Jackson Turner, "The Significance of History," in *Rereading Frederick Jackson Turner: "The Significance of the Frontier in History" and Other Essays*, ed. John Mack Faragher, (New York, NY: Henry Holt, 1991) 18.

6 Frederick Jackson Turner, *The Significance of Sections in American History*, ed. Max Farrand (New York, NY: Henry Holt, 1932). iii–x.

7 Marnie Hughes-Warrington, "Frederick Jackson Turner (1861–1932)," in *Fifty Key Thinkers on History* (London: Routledge, 2000), 335.

8 Billington, *Frederick Jackson Turner*, 345–8.

9 Ernst Breisach, *American Progressive History: An Experiment in Modernization* (Chicago, IL: Chicago UP, 1993), 63–4.

10 Daniel T. Rodgers, "Exceptionalism," in *Imagined Histories: American Historians Interpret the Past*, eds. Gordon Wood and Anthony Molho (Princeton, NJ: Princeton UP, 1998), 34–5.

11 Faragher, ed., *Rereading Frederick Jackson Turner,* 1.

12 Faragher, ed., *Rereading Frederick Jackson Turner*, 3.

13 Breisach, *American Progressive History*, 1.

14 Billington, *Frederick Jackson Turner*, 237–8.

SECTION 3
IMPACT

MODULE 9
THE FIRST RESPONSES

KEY POINTS

- Turner's critics alleged his use of the term "frontier"* was vague; that he ignored both the violence and reality of life on the frontier.
- Turner never responded directly to these criticisms, but later shifted his attention to social history.
- The growing plurality of American society played the biggest role in shaping responses to Turner's work.

Criticism

On first publication in 1893, Turner's "The Significance of the Frontier" made little impact. American author and historian Edward Everett Hale* described it as a "curious and interesting paper."[1] Similarly, the future president Theodore Roosevelt* responded that Turner had "struck some first class ideas" but went no further, suggesting his interest in Turner's work was short-lived and bordered on indifference.[2] In other words, these leading historians passed over Turner's work. This was indirectly damning, because it shunned Turner's ideas in the same way that historians resisted the work of sexologists,* ethnographers, and sociologists who were showing how people's behavior on the new soil of America transformed them into Americans with their own sexual, ethnic, and social dynamics.[3] But the initial indifference to his thesis did not set back Turner's professional reputation. Within 20 years of publication of "The Significance of the Frontier" Turner had enough support to be elected president of the American Historical Association.*

> ❝ Even Turner's sharpest critics have rarely failed to concede the core merits of his thesis, and wisely so. For over two hundred and fifty years the American people shaped their lives with the vast, empty interior of the continent before them. Their national experience up to Turner's day had been involved with conquering, securing, occupying, and developing their continental empire. ❞
>
> Richard Hofstadter, *The Progressive Historians: Turner, Beard, Parrington*

Criticism of Turner's work became more explicit following World War I.* A younger generation was less positive about the course of world history that had led to the rise of the modern USA. And they saw the frontier as the opposite of Turner's space where liberation and development flourished. One of Turner's critics, American philosopher, psychologist, and educational reformer John Dewey,* argued that the frontier restricted freedom of speech rather than promoting democracy.[4] Turner's thesis was based on the notion that white settlers travelling West took advantage of the vast reserves of free land to forge new lives. But one historian of the 1920s, Paul Wallace Gates,* believed Turner had overlooked Native American* communities that had legitimate rights to the land.[5] Turner's claim that land was "free" led him to ignore the brutality and injustice that accompanied European settlement in the West.[6]

Historians of America also continued to reject the frontier as the key element in American history. Roosevelt emphasized the importance of European institutions in forming America's own.[7] This matched debates in Europe, for example in England where historians traced the relationship between the US Supreme Court and the UK Parliament.[8] Supporters of the New History,* such as Charles Beard,* also looked to sidestep the frontier as the dominating factor that formed America. Beard preferred to argue that the Pilgrim Fathers* operated for their own economic benefit in writing and ratifying the US Constitution.[9]

Responses

Despite the criticism that emerged in the last decade of his life, Turner held firm. He responded that his critics had failed to understand the breadth and complexity of ideas in "The Significance of the Frontier." In response to John Dewey—who argued that the frontier restricted freedom and democracy—Turner pointed out that the essay had indeed cautioned that the frontier experience did not always have positive results. This included the excess of individualism that became anti-social.[10] Turner had argued that life on the frontier bred traits of selfishness, corruption, and anarchy. And he dismissed Charles Beard outright when he argued that class conflict between capitalists (those who owned businesses) and laborers drove American history. Turner characterized Beard as a left-wing radical who was mistaken in thinking that economics acted as the sole instigator of historical events, in the manner of a Marxist.*[11]

Turner's interest was, nevertheless, captured by the world economic turmoil created by World War I* that had prompted Beard's thinking. This change of direction resulted from disheartening rejections of Turner's frontier thesis at the highest levels of academia and government; Woodrow Wilson,* Turner's friend and the future President, dismissed his frontier thesis without comment.[12] The stock market instability of 1914 and the post-war difficulties of the 1920s affected the ability of ordinary Americans to buy basic consumer goods, such as food and fuel. As a result, many workers became disheartened and went on strike in protest at their declining living standards.[13] So Turner switched his focus to social and regional history, which he "had done more than any other individual to stimulate,"[14] in this period as a response to the social and economic crisis in America. His essay "Sections and Nation" reflected his new focus on how local interests created American life.[15] But this response did not alter the frontier thesis itself. Rather, Turner recast his historical understanding to fit historical events in ways that the public and historians would accept.[16]

Conflict And Consensus

Because Turner and his critics effectively passed each other as ships in the night, neither side directly confronted the other and modified their views as a result. The challenge to Turner's work came later in the twentieth century when his presumptions about white seizure and negotiation with Native Americans, and his idea of the frontier as an area where Americans developed their particularly American way of life, came under fierce scrutiny.

NOTES

1 Ray Allen Billington, *The Genesis of the Frontier Thesis: A Study in Historical Creativity* (San Marino, CA: Huntington Library, 1971), 13.

2 Billington, *Genesis of the Frontier Thesis*, 13–14.

3 Peter Boag, *Re-dressing America's Frontier Past* (Berkeley, CA: California UP, 2011), 199 n.10.

4 John Dewey, *Democracy and Education* (New York: Henry Holt, 1914), 88.

5 Paul Wallace Gates, *Fifty Million Acres: Conflicts Over Kansas Land Policy, 1854–1890* (New York, NY: Arno Press, 1954).

6 Gates, *Fifty Million Acres*, 56.

7 Thomas C. Reeves, *Twentieth-Century America: A Brief History* (Oxford: Oxford UP, 2000), 28–31.

8 Michael Bentley, *Modernizing England's Past: English Historiography in the Age of Modernism 1870–1970* (Cambridge: Cambridge, UP, 2005), 35–6.

9   Gerald D. Nash, *Creating the West: Historical Interpretations 1890–1990* (Albuquerque: University of New Mexico Press, 1991), 24, 34, 95.

10 Frederick Jackson Turner, "The Significance of the Frontier in American History," in *The Frontier in American History* (New York: Holt, 1921), 36.

11 Ray Allen Billington, *Frederick Jackson Turner: Historian, Scholar, Teacher* (Oxford: Oxford UP, 1973),, 532 n. 32.

12 Nash, *Creating the West*, 18.

13 Reeves, *Twentieth-Century America*, 126, 140, 156.

14 Nash, *Creating the West*, 52.

15 Frederick Jackson Turner, *The Significance of Sections in American History*, ed. Max Farrand (New York, NY: Henry Holt, 1932), i–xii.

16 Ernst Breisach, *American Progressive History: An Experiment in Modernization* (Chicago, IL: Chicago UP, 1993), 28.

MODULE 10
THE EVOLVING DEBATE

KEY POINTS

- Turner's essay founded three new branches of historical research: agricultural history, environmental history, and Western history.
- "The Significance of the Frontier" contributed to the rise of the New History.*
- Turner's work has had a lasting impact in stimulating research on borderlands* inside and outside America.

Uses And Problems

Frederick Jackson Turner's "The Significance of the Frontier" didn't just serve as a historical document of its time. It made history in its own right, founding the field of American Western History. Later debates in the field responded to Turner's work, supporting or questioning it. This strand of scholarship continues to the present and became the subject of professional specialism from the 1960s onward. It can be seen in the Western History Association* and its quarterly magazine, *The American West Magazine*—and more recently in the periodical, the *American West Quarterly*.[1] Into the 1970s scholars working in this tradition studied aspects of the frontier and the geography of the West in close detail. They have focused on areas such as the history of America's national parks—enclosures preserving some of America's vast, unsettled areas.[2] Today, the Association continues to award prizes and scholarships to those excelling in Western history.[3]

A critique of the frontier* thesis from various opponents developed alongside the growth of Western history. At Turner's death in 1932, critics

> **"** If frontiers are what happens when cultures collide and attempt to work out ways to work together, the postwar period deserves prominence in the annals of American frontier history. Not only were Native Americans* resurgent, but Mexican Americans and African Americans mounted an impressive challenge to the ethnic and racial order that had been established during the nineteenth century—the dual labor system, the segregation of minorities, and their exclusion from the political system. **"**
>
> John Mack Farragher, *Rereading Frederick Jackson Turner*

reacted against the vagueness of his language and the lack of cited evidence in his essays. George W. Pierson* and historian Richard Hofstadter* captured the core of these criticisms. They argued that Turner used "frontier" to mean different things, so the point of the "frontier thesis" was not clear.[4] This was not merely nitpicking, as Turner used the word "frontier" to signal different concepts and places: "the edge of settled territory," "the line of settlement," and "the West"—as well as "a process" and "a form of society."[5] Hofstadter's colleague in the promotion of the New History,* Charles Beard,* argued that the frontier did not explain the rise of slavery on Southern plantations. He maintained that only an economic history of America would reveal the reasons for slavery.[6] In turn, political scientist Benjamin Wright* argued the opposite of Turner: that the culture, society, and ethnic make-up of East Coast cities such as Boston and New York determined life in the West; that Americans settled there first and then exported their settlement patterns westward.[7]

Schools Of Thought

Whether they agreed with him or not, Turner's work paved the way for Beard, Hofstadter, and others and inspired them to create the New

History. New Historians wanted to use objective, scientific history to identify the problems and experiences of the population at large in different national societies.[8] American New History therefore looked at the experiences and contributions to national life of ordinary Americans on their own terms. It not only examined their differences and individual natures but also how, when taken together, they created American national life.[9]

During the Great Depression* of the 1930s, Beard's argument that the Pilgrim Fathers* founded America for their own economic benefit chimed with a popular mood. Americans were angry with bankers who took the blame for creating the world's most serious stock market crash prior to 2008.[10] By the 1950s, a new age of liberal reform and economic prosperity had gained a foothold in America. New History gave way to interpretations of America's social and cultural history that emphasized consensus. American political scientist Louis Hartz* argued that a general liberal agreement about free-market capitalism* (in which trade and industry are owned by private individuals rather than the state) and political democracy determined the course of the nation's development.[11] Turner's essay spoke of the "West" as a constantly moving boundary line that shifted each time social development occurred. And so a classic debate arose: was the West a process or a place?

More recently, Turner's work has formed the foundation of two additional subfields: environmental history and agricultural history, which emerged primarily in the 1980s. Environmental history's best-known practitioner, William Cronon,* openly acknowledges a major debt to Turner. Through his groundbreaking work, Turner was the first historian to recognize that a relationship between the land and the people had historical consequences.[12] Environmental history attempts to discover how the natural world has shaped human events. Rather than people being the prime actors in human history, their role becomes limited by a world they have few powers to control.[13] Agricultural history deepens the study of this relationship between man and nature. It reveals how the food supply—along with weather and other conditions that affect it—has exerted pressure on population growth. Notably this includes how societies try to transform themselves in conditions of drought and adversity.[14]

In Current Scholarship

Recent scholarship has reevaluated Turner's work—with mixed degrees of enthusiasm. New Western historians such as Patricia Nelson Limerick* argue that scholars like Turner view the West as a process rather than a place. She believes that Turner overlooked the histories of people and communities rooted in specific places.[15] However, in Turner's broader body of work it can be seen that he initiated the idea of the West as a region.[16] In 1922, Turner wrote, "There is no more enduring, no more influential force in our history than the formation and interplay of the different regions of the United States."[17] By recognizing the duality of the West—that it is both a geographical space and a concept of change over time—scholars can move on to answer questions about the Western United States that are relevant to current debates about the environment, the use of resources, and the role of the federal government in economic development.[18]

Lacy K. Ford* is a prominent scholar who supports many of Turner's arguments. In his assessment of census records and other data, he found that the frontier indeed provided greater economic opportunity for many Americans. It also acted as a safety valve for democracy (though to a lesser extent than Turner claimed) by staving off a sectional conflict between the North and South until the right to vote had sufficiently expanded to include most white men.[19]

Although William Cronon does not support the specifics of Turner's frontier thesis, he finds value in Turner's argument about the formative experience of American interactions with Native Americans. In particular he pays attention to the relationship between ethnic groups and their environment. His first book, *Changes in the Land: Indians, Colonists, and the Ecology of New England* (1983), argued that Native Americans did not live passively in the wilderness as many historians had assumed but actively shaped the environment.[20] In *Nature's Metropolis: Chicago and the Great West*, Cronon further expanded upon this idea of relationships with the environment, looking at how mechanized farming enabled the growth of America's towns. Unlike Turner, he does not analyze the frontier and the city as separate entities but as interdependent parts of the national economy.[21]

But the frontier as a concept has not disappeared. Historians Robert Hine* and John Mack Faragher* argue that the frontier remains too central to the American psyche to ignore. It is more than just a place: symbolically the frontier represents (accurately or not) freedom, opportunity, and the individual spirit. They suggest the plural noun "frontiers" as a way to retain the essence of Turner's idea, while replacing his national identity with one that incorporates a variety of cultures and ethnicities well-suited to modern-American society.[22] In addition, historians of the American West use terms such as "borderlands,"* "contact zones,"* or "middle ground," that emerged out of dissatisfaction with the limitations of "frontier."[23] Nevertheless, all of these terms derive from Turner's basic frontier concept.

NOTES

1   For further information on all their activities, see http://www.westernhistoryassociation.wildapricot.org/.

2   Robert M. Utley, "Yellowstone and the National Park Concept, 1872–1972," and Phillip D. Thomas, "The Near Extinction of the Bison: A Case Study in Legislative Lethargy," in *Western American History in the Seventies: Selected Papers Presented to the First Western History Conference, Colorado State University, August 10–12, 1972*, ed. Daniel Tyler (Fort Collins, CO: Robinson for Educational Media & Information Systems, 1972), 7–13, 121–35.

3   See "Book Awards," http://www.westernhistoryassociation.wildapricot.org/awards/books.

4   George W. Pierson, "The Frontier and the Frontiersmen of Turner's Essay," *Pennsylvania Magazine of History and Biography* 64, no. 4 (1940): 449–78; Richard Hofstadter, "Turner and the Frontier Myth," *American Scholar* 18, no. 4 (1949): 433–43.

5   Frederick Jackson Turner, "The Significance of the Frontier in American History," in *The Frontier in American History* (New York: Holt, 1921), 1, 3, 5, 10.

6   Richard White, "*It's Your Misfortune and None of My Own:*" A History of the American West (Norman, OK: Oklahoma UP, 1991), 613–32.

7   White, "*It's Your Misfortune*", 321.

8   Ernst Breisach, *American Progressive History: An Experiment in Modernization* (Chicago, IL: Chicago UP, 1993), 3.

9   Breisach, *American Progressive History*, 66–7.

10   Breisach, *American Progressive History*, 95.

11   Charles A. Beard and Mary Ritter Beard, *The Rise of American Civilization* (New York, NY: Macmillan, 1927); Louis Hartz, *The Liberal Tradition in America: An Interpretation of American Political Thought since the Revolution* (New York, BY: Harcourt, 1955).

12   William Cronon, "Revisiting the Vanishing Frontier: The Legacy of Frederick Jackson Turner," *Western Historical Quarterly* 18, no. 2 (1987): 171.

13   Frank Uekoetter, "Thinking Big: The Broad Outlines of a Burgeoning Field," in *The Turning Points of Environmental History*, ed. Frank Uekoetter (Pittsburgh, PA: Pittsburgh UP, 2010), 1–12.

14   R. Douglas Hurt, "Reflections on American Agricultural History," *The Agricultural History Review* 52, no. 1 (2004): 1–19.

15   Patricia Nelson Limerick, *The Legacy of Conquest: The Unbroken Past of the American West* (New York: Norton, 1988), 21, 71, 84.

16   Michael Steiner, "From Frontier to Region: Frederick Jackson Turner and the New Western History," *Pacific Historical Review* 64, no. 4 (1995): 481.

17   Quoted in Steiner, "From Frontier to Region," 486.

18   Karen J. Leong, "Still Walking, Still Brave: Mapping Gender, Race, and Power in U.S. Western History," *Pacific Historical Review* 79, no. 4 (2010): 618–28.

19 Lacy K. Ford Jr., "Frontier Democracy: The Turner Thesis Revisited." *Journal of the Early Republic* 13, no. 2 (1993): 62, 63, 155.

20 William Cronon, *Changes in the Land: Indians, Colonists, and the Ecology of New England* (New York: Hill and Wang, 1983).

21 William Cronon, *Nature's Metropolis: Chicago and the Great West* (New York: W.W. Norton, 1991).

22 Robert V. Hine and John Mack Faragher, *Frontiers: A Short History of the American West* (New Haven: Yale University Press, 2007).

23 See Herbert Eugene Bolton, *The Spanish Borderlands: A Chronicle of Old Florida and the Southwest* (Albuquerque: University of New Mexico Press, 1996 (1921)); Richard White, *The Middle Ground: Indians, Empires, and Republics in the Great Lakes Region, 1650–1815* (New York: Cambridge University Press, 1991).

IMPACT AND INFLUENCE TODAY

KEY POINTS

- "The Significance of the Frontier" is a classic text today.
- Transnational* and global history have challenged the importance of borders and frontiers.
- Western historians and scholars of gender and sexuality use the frontier concept in multiple ways, not just in the geographical sense.

Position

Frederick Jackson Turner's "The Significance of the Frontier" remains a classic. Its interpretation of American history is still explored today and endures as a popular historical essay inside and outside academia. Into the 1990s, William Cronon* argued, Turner's explanation of the formation of America in terms of Americans living on the frontier* retained "remarkable explanatory power."[1] This stemmed from the continued presence of Turner's frontier thesis, not only among Western historians but also American historians more generally. This conclusion still carries weight more than 100 years after Turner's essay emerged. John Mack Faragher's* editorial work that produced the re-edition of Turner's works, *Rereading Frederick Jackson Turner*, starts with "The Significance of the Frontier," just as Turner's own essay collection did in 1920.[2]

Yet the force of Turner's frontier concept—in which Americans forged a unique history separate from Europe—has diminished. In the twenty-first century, American history focuses not on United States expansion across North America, but rather on "America in

> **"**The New Western History developed alongside another movement in the historical profession: public history.**"**
>
> Douglas W. Wood, "Introduction," *The Public Historian*

the world."[3] Scholars seek to understand how transnational trade, international migration patterns, and ocean-crossing intellectual and cultural currents have shaped American history. This challenges Turner's model of a self-contained nation-state.[4] In addition, more historians use the concept of borderlands,* coined by Turner's student Herbert Eugene Bolton* in 1921, rather than frontiers to describe zones of contact and conflict between different cultural groups.[5]

Interaction

Even if Turner's concept of the frontier has been reformed or replaced, it still remains. School- and college-level history teaching bases itself on texts that follow the model outlined by Turner. First there were Native Americans,* then traders, then farmers, then urbanized settlements.[6] Yet virtually all scholars agree that Turner's work suffered from flaws that reflect a nineteenth-century world view that is now outdated.[7]

Rather than seeing the frontier as a clash between European civilization and the savagery of the untamed wilderness, most New Western historians now see it as a contact zone* in which different factions and forces compete for power. Robert Hine* and John Mack Faragher* speak of multiple frontiers to emphasize this plurality—and to mix good and bad features of a frontier life often as violent and destructive as formative.[8]

This model of understanding American history also continues to show itself in popular imaginings of the American West. Television shows, films, and novels showcase white settlers travelling westward and clashing with Native Americans. Although figures such as William "Buffalo Bill" Cody* romanticized the Western frontier years before the 1893 essay, Turner's use of the frontier concept in historical scholarship gave it legitimacy in intellectual and political public spheres. When John F. Kennedy* ran for President in 1960, he called his political platform the "New Frontier."[9] Columbia University requires all undergraduates to take a course titled "Frontiers of Science."[10] The "frontier" remains a concept with the same meaning Turner gave it in his essay: a space for opportunity, possibility, and optimism.

The Continuing Debate

As a postmodern* approach to history became more prominent, with its focus on everyday people—women, slaves, ethnic minorities—attention turned away from Turner's view of the American past. Critics of "The Significance of the Frontier" point to the things he left out. He does not include women and gives no voice to Native Americans; nor does he acknowledge the presence in the West of African Americans, Chinese Americans, or Mexican Americans. His sweeping assessment of frontier development proves false when examining regional communities.[11]

In 1993, the centennial year of Turner's "The Significance of the Frontier," several historians defended his frontier thesis in a special issue of the *Journal of the Early Republic*.[12] They argued that much was gained by viewing the American West as a process of development, rather than merely as a place. But, since then, historians of the American West now generally see the West as both. They have moved on to other questions, such as the influence of global migration patterns and international trade.[13] Turner's work lives on but decreases in importance.

Recent moves towards transnational and global history both challenge and adopt Turner's ideas. As it gains in popularity, transnational history exposes flaws in Turner's approach. It shows how hard it is to understand American history without considering regional and political connections across borders, even those as close as with Canada.[14] Since the 1990s, on the other hand, the increasingly popular field of global history has renewed a call to examine history's big picture—making Turner relevant again. Turner saw a global aspect in the frontier because to him American life there represented the most advanced stage of human civilization in the world.[15] Global historians rejected this idea but seized on the scale of Turner's work and, like him, they asked big questions about world history across the globe. Turner's ability to ask large questions and demand broad syntheses challenges scholars today to think outside super-specialized subfields. Though historians often criticize Jared Diamond's* 1997 book, *Guns, Germs, and Steel*, the volume was a popular bestseller because it dared to answer a big question that Turner addressed in his essay: what is the relationship between geography and human destiny?[16]

Turner's ideas still shape American history textbooks and several current debates in American Western history. Most texts still discuss "westward expansion" as a process in which European settlers marched across the continent, conquering the frontier and Native American tribes. And, albeit in modified form, twenty-first century historians still use his concept of the "frontier."

Another major challenge has come from those engaged with Native American history, particularly American historians Richard White* and David Richter.* White's concept of the "middle ground"—a zone where Native Americans and Europeans met and created a common culture—in some ways echoes Turner. But, unlike Turner, White does not view Native Americans as savages or victims of annihilation. He sees them as politically and economically motivated actors who played a central role in creating this new culture.[17] To counter Turner's westward point of view, David Richter calls for scholars to consider American history from the eyes of those "facing East," such as Native Americans, who faced the arrival of European and American settlers.[1]

NOTES

1   William Cronon, "Revisiting the Vanishing Frontier: The Legacy of Frederick Jackson Turner," *Western Historical Quarterly* 18, no. 2 (1987): 160.

2   John Mack Faragher, ed., *Rereading Frederick Jackson Turner: "The Significance of the Frontier in History" and Other Essays* (New York, NY: Henry Holt, 1991), 31–60.

3   Thomas Bender, "Historians, the Nation and the Plenitude of Narratives," in *Rethinking American History in a Global Age* (Berkeley, CA: California UP, 2002), 1–22.

4   Karen Ordahl Kupperman, "International at the Creation: Early American History," in *Rethinking American History*, 103–48.

5   For more on the current state of concepts of the frontier and borderlands, see Stephen Aron, "Frontiers, Borderlands, Wests," in *American History Now*, eds. Eric Foner and Lisa McGirr (Philadelphia: Temple University Press, 2011), 263–86.

6   George Brown Tindall and David Emory Shi, *America: A Narrative History* (New York: Norton, 2007).

7   Faragher, *Rereading Frederick Jackson Turner*, 6–9.

8   Robert V. Hine and John Mack Faragher, *Frontiers: A Short History of the American West* (New Haven: Yale University Press, 2007).

9   Thomas C. Reeves, *Twentieth-Century America: A Brief History* (Oxford: Oxford UP, 2000), 171.

10 Nicholas Christie-Black, "Core Curriculum: Frontiers of Science," http://www.college.columbia.edu/core/classes/fos.php.

11 Glenda Riley, "Frederick Jackson Turner Overlooked the Ladies," *Journal of the Early Republic* 13, no. 2 (1993): 216–30.

12 Martin Ridge, "Turner the Historian: A Long Shadow," *Journal of the Early Republic* 13, no. 2 (1993): 133–44.

13 For example, Keith R. Widder, *Beyond Pontiac's Shadow: Michilimackinac and the Anglo-Indian War of 1763* (East Lansing, MI: Michigan State University Press, 2013).

14 Benjamin Johnson and Andrew R. Graybill, eds., *Bridging National Borders in North America* (Durham, NC: Duke UP, 2010), 2–6.

15 Frederick Jackson Turner, "The Significance of the Frontier in American History," in *The Frontier in American History* (New York: Holt, 1921), 37.

16 Turner, "The Significance of the Frontier," 38 and "The Significance of History," in *Rereading Frederick Jackson Turner*, 16.

17 Richard White, *The Middle Ground: Indians, Empires, and Republics in the Great Lakes Region, 1650–1815* (New York: Cambridge University Press, 1991).

18 Daniel K. Richter, *Facing East from Indian Country: A Native History of Early America* (Cambridge, MA: Harvard University Press, 2001).

WHERE NEXT?

KEY POINTS

- "The Significance of the Frontier" will continue to promote global research in cross-border exchange.

- It will exert this influence because it has become a celebrated work of American history and is widely known internationally.

- "The Significance of the Frontier" is a key text because of the model of historical writing it presents, because it sowed the seeds for new directions in American history writing, and because it puts forward concepts still current in American society and politics today.

Potential

Though Frederick Jackson Turner's "The Significance of the Frontier" attempted to explain specific forces that shaped the American character, his frontier* concept now stimulates debate worldwide. Historians of settler nations*—where European settlers, rather than indigenous inhabitants, established formal governments— have found the frontier idea extremely useful. Scholars from many fields and disciplines utilized both Turner's "frontier" and the concept of "borderlands"* coined by his student Herbert Eugene Bolton* to analyze non-geographic phenomena. Chicana* feminist scholar Gloria Anzaldúa,* for example, uses "borderlands"* and "la frontera" (the frontier) in social analysis. She argues that invisible borders operate in social relations. These change and adapt so that gender identities, sexuality, and politics evolve as the roles of men and women change in Mexican society.[1]

> ❝How so metaphoric an essay as Turner's 'The Significance of the Frontier in American History' should have established itself as the most important single piece of historical writing to come out of the late-nineteenth century United States can scarcely be comprehended outside the popular convictions Turner's word pictures caught so well.❞
>
> Daniel T. Rodgers, "Exceptionalism"

In studying settler nations such as Australia, Argentina, Canada, South Africa, and Israel, historians have found the frontier concept particularly useful when analyzing the interactions between European settlers and indigenous groups.[2] Others utilize Turner's focus on the way environmental and human factors combine to create distinct national identities. As historian of Russia Mark Bassin* put it, "Movement into and across open continental spaces [...] has been quite as central to the historical experience of a variety of other nations as it was in the United States."[3]

The story of the American West continues to chime with popular culture. Turner's frontier thesis parallels the "culture wars" in twenty-first century United States. Academics, public intellectuals, and those with a center-left political viewpoint generally adopt a multicultural historical perspective. This acknowledges the negative impact of European settlement on other ethnic groups in the Americas and is in general more critical of westward expansion.[4] Those on the center-right or conservative end of the political spectrum argue that such revisions of American history are unnecessarily negative—and in fact, un-American. Thus Arizona passed a law in 2010 that banned public schools from offering ethnic studies courses, particularly Mexican American studies. The reasoning was that such courses promoted resentment of white Americans.[5]

Turner's vision of the frontier as a space that provides opportunity and freedom is one that many outside of academic circles still hold true, despite almost universal agreement within academia that his viewpoint is too narrow-minded and celebratory for the twenty-first century.[6]

Future Directions

Though the American West closed its frontier long ago, Turner's frontier thesis will continue to expand in impact, if not directly but by means of the seeds it planted. These include interpretations of American history and global work on borderlands* and frontiers. The content of "The Significance of the Frontier" will not attract attention in and of itself: it simply cannot accommodate important new studies of ethnicity and gender. After the explosion of Chicano* Studies, Native American* Studies, Women's Studies, and other programs in the 1960s, few historians have written about the West without recognizing multiethnic influences. At the same time, students of United States history continue to read Turner's essay to grasp the basics of scholarship on the American West. Any student of borderlands, contact zones,* or frontiers remains, in part, indebted to his work.[7]

Public history informing Americans about their past will still draw inspiration from Turner, though less so than before. Newer models that emphasize the multicultural roots of the American experience have made inroads into popular culture. Nevertheless, they have failed to dislodge Turner's positive view of frontier expansion. Historian Stephen Aron* points to the 2004–5 Lewis and Clark Bicentennial Celebrations as an example of current popular views on westward expansion. Exhibits and media commemorating Lewis and Clark's journey* highlighted the roles of Sacajawea,* the expedition's female Indian guide, and York,* an African American slave. These inclusions point to the multicultural turn in Western

American history; previous celebrations of the journey largely ignored women and African Americans. At the same time, the 2004–5 public exhibitions refused to adopt recent scholarship's focus on the exploitation and bloodshed that accompanied westward expansion.[8] The exhibits instead celebrated the promise, excitement, and opportunities that the frontier afforded. The global public continues to imagine an American West largely along the lines Turner depicted. But that, too, will perhaps slowly change.

Summary

"The Significance of the Frontier" altered how American historians understood America's past and initiated three new subdisciplines in history: agricultural, environmental, and Western history. For 20 years, Turner's interpretation of the frontier's importance in American democracy and national character went mostly unchallenged. Though criticism of his thesis mounted after World War I,* historians of the American West still could not imagine models of historical change without the frontier.

Debates that emerged in the 1980s and 1990s about the American West as either a process or a place demonstrated the relevance of Turner's work. Few historians could escape the power of his overarching narrative of American development, or create such a well-synthesized understanding of American history.

With the change of course to transnational* and global history, Turner's impact has lessened. Now historians turn to multiple frontiers, borderlands, and Wests, emphasizing the wide range of experiences and historical developments that occurred in the geographic region now considered the Western part of the United States.

The general public, however, still appreciates straightforward narratives. Turner's linear explanation of American development from East to West satisfies popular longing for an origin story. His vision of the West remains part of America's popular imagination. There he saw clashes between civilization and savagery that bred distinct American characteristics of individualism and pragmatism. There he witnessed an expanding westward frontier that provided vast economic opportunities.

"The Significance of the Frontier in American History" yielded riches of a different sort: a new theory and a way of thinking that enriched all historians who came after him. Some built on his ideas; others took issue with his limited scope and prejudices. Nevertheless, all are indebted to Frederick Jackson Turner and his seminal work.

NOTES

1   Gloria Anzaldúa, *Borderlands/La Frontera: The New Mestiza* (San Francisco, CA: Aunt Lute Books, 1987).

2   Julie Evans et al., "Sovereignty," in *Sovereignty: Frontiers of Possibility* (Honolulu, HI: Hawaii UP, 2012), 1–16.

3   Mark Bassin, "Turner, Solov'ev, and The 'Frontier Hypothesis': The Nationalist Signification of Open Spaces," *Journal of Modern History* 65, no. 3 (1993): 473.

4   Daniel T. Rodgers, *Age of Fracture* (Cambridge, MA: Harvard UP, 2011), 256–60.

5   Fernanda Santos, "Arizona: Most of Law on Ethnic Studies is Upheld," *New York Times,* March 11, 2013, accessed March 1, 2015, http://www. nytimes.com/2013/03/12/education/most-of-arizona-law-on-ethnic-studies-is-upheld.html?_r=0.

6   Patricia L. Limerick, "The Adventures of the Frontier in the Twentieth Century," in *The Frontier in American Culture*, ed. James R. Grossman (Berkeley, CA: California UP, 1994), 67–102.

7   John Mack Faragher, ed., *Rereading Frederick Jackson Turner: "The Significance of the Frontier in History" and Other Essays* (New York, NY: Henry Holt, 1991), 3.

8   Stephen Aron, "Frontiers, Borderlands, Wests," in *American History Now*, eds. Eric Foner and Lisa McGirr (Philadelphia: Temple University Press, 2011), 262.

GLOSSARIES

GLOSSARY OF TERMS

American Civil War (1861–65): the immediate cause of the conflict was over the expansion of slavery in the US and over cotton and other trading between the states. Thirteen Southern states formed the Confederate States and declared their independence after the election of President Abraham Lincoln, who led the Unionist states in the North.

American Historical Association: founded in 1884, this is a professional body of which many historians in America are members. Their role is to lobby government on, and promote generally, historical education, preservation of records and manuscripts with historical value in the US, and to preserve access to those records for the public at large and for historians.

Anglo-Saxon: an ethnic group inhabiting England from the fifth century up until the Norman invasion in 1066. The term is used to describe the many descendants of that race, characteristically people of the English-speaking, or Anglophone, world in Great Britain, North America, and Australia.

Borderlands: borderlands are worldwide phenomena in which various institutional presences—national governments, industrial and social formations, warfare, communications technology, and the growth of cities among others—attempted to establish borders, thus forming the basis for a myriad of reactions, counter-reactions, and interactions.

Capitalism: an economic system in which trade and industry are owned by private individuals rather than the state.

Chicana: a woman of Mexican origin or descent living in the United States of America.

Cold War: hostilities not involving armed conflict between the forces of the United States and the USSR between approximately 1945 and 1989. It included threats, violent propaganda, espionage, and often the potential of mutual destruction by nuclear weapons.

Contact zones: the term "contact zone" became widespread in the 1990s to signify a new, holistic approach to what historians previously called the frontier. Contact zones are studied as complex wholes, requiring scholars to look at social, political, geographical, economic, and intellectual aspects of life.

Congress of Albany of 1754: a meeting of French and English colonists with Native Americans in Albany, New York, to try to set up a "general government" to manage relations with the Native Americans and French. Though the delegates of the "Albany Congress," as it was called, unanimously passed the "Albany Plan," the colonial legislatures rejected it, fearing an encroachment upon their powers.

Evolutionary biology: the study of how organisms evolved, a field founded by the English naturalist Charles Darwin, who wrote *On the Origin of Species*, in which he posited that life forms evolved into new species over time from less-developed life forms. Many people believed that the idea of evolution was heretical because it challenged the version of creation as told in the Bible.

Exceptionalism: the concept that America differs from the rest of the world; its history revealing a different, better path than that taken by other nations.

Frontier: the geographical boundary between the settled territories in the East and the American territories not settled by Europeans and their descendants in the West. The frontier moved westwards with the arrival of settlers as they built farms, towns, and cities in America until settlement was completed in the 1890s.

Germ theory: a theory posited by Herbert Baxter Adams* who compared the growth of social patterns with the transmission of illness between people by the spread of germs, or bacteria.

Great Depression: a period of falling wages and decreasing productivity producing no economic growth, beginning with the Wall Street Crash of 1929.

Interdisciplinary history: interdisciplinary history represents a methodological school of thought among historians promoting the use of techniques from all other subjects rather than narrow documentary techniques to further our understanding of the past.

Lewis and Clark's journey: Meriwether Lewis (1774–1809) and William Clark (1770–1838) were two explorers whom President Thomas Jefferson commissioned in 1804 to explore the vast, unincorporated area of the American West that Jefferson had just purchased from the French (known as "the Louisiana Purchase").

Marxist: an approach to historical study or any other pursuit based on Marxism, the writings and methods of German philosopher Karl Marx (1818–83) which found events in all aspects of life to be the result of economic forces that determined human behavior.

Middle Atlantic: the Middle Atlantic section of the United States consists of states such as Pennsylvania, New York, and New Jersey, which were settled by diverse groups of people in the initial colonial period of the seventeenth and early eighteenth centuries.

Nationalism: the belief in loyalty, often fiercely held, to the identity, culture, economy, and other features of one's nation-state.

Native Americans: members of the numerous tribes and indigenous peoples living in North America at the time when European settlers arrived in the seventeenth century, prior to the formation of the United States of America. These peoples are sometimes referred to as indigenous Americans.

New History: a movement beginning around 1910 led by Charles Beard and his colleagues across America, particularly James Harvey Robinson in New York City. New History maintained that history should focus increasingly on the mass of the American people not considered in the grand narratives of America's colonization by Europeans.

Panic of 1893: a downturn in the American economy that lasted for four years and had a variety of causes, including the overbuilding of railroads and a run on the silver supply. It was the largest economic depression to that date in the United States, in which hundreds of banks and thousands of businesses failed.

Pilgrim Fathers: the group of English Puritans who set up the colony of Plymouth, Massachusetts, in 1620 and are regarded as the founders of the modern United States. (*OED*)

Positivism: in historical studies, the body of thought that insists the role of historians is to extract facts from evidence, to verify that these facts are correct by checking as many written sources as possible and then to insert these facts into a linear, often narrative account, of the subject they are studying. Positivism mimics the approach of laboratory and natural scientists.

Postmodernism: in the study of history, a climate of opinion after the 1970s that modern approaches to history did not explain the past convincingly. It rejected science and institutions as suitable ways to relate past events to contemporary readers, instead focusing on the points of view and experiences of under-represented groups in society such as women, ethnic minorities, and homosexuals.

Puritan: a movement of English Protestants in the late-sixteenth and seventeenth centuries. They were looking to remove all traces of Roman Catholic Church practice that remained after the Protestant Reformation and which they considered to be unscriptural, idolatrous, or corrupt.

Republican: one of the two major political parties in the USA, founded in 1854 by anti-slavery activists. They base their party policies on American conservatism as opposed to the liberal politics of the American Democratic Party.

Settler nations: countries where European settlers, rather than indigenous inhabitants, established formal governments.

Sexology: the interdisciplinary study of human sexuality, broadly conceived as encompassing sexual orientation, sexual behavior, and sexual function.

Transnationalism: in historical studies, the growing body of scholarship on methodology requiring historians to isolate one phenomena in two or more countries and identify how they interacted across national borders over time. An example would be working-class movements in Germany and the USA.

Western History Association: founded in 1961 in Santa Fe, New Mexico, but now headquartered in Fairbanks, Alaska, the Association devotes itself to the promotion and support of scholars and students studying the history of America's West.

World War I: worldwide armed conflict lasting from 1914 until 1918 (with some variation depending on which country was concerned; America only entered the war in 1917). Centered in Europe, the conflict involved the major economic world powers of the day.

PEOPLE MENTIONED IN THE TEXT

George Burton Adams (1851–1925) was an American medieval historian who played an important role in founding the *American Historical Review*. In his later career he argued with progressive historians over the use of social science methods, preferring science and political history to New History,* as in *A Constitutional History of England* (1921).

Herbert Baxter Adams (1850–1901) was an American historian of America who taught at Johns Hopkins University where he introduced students, including Turner, to the idea of studying history scientifically. He is best known for *The Germanic Origin of the New England Towns* (1882).

William F. Allen (1830–89) was an American medievalist and educational reformer who spent the entirety of his career at the University of Wisconsin. His notable works include *Higher Education in Wisconsin* (1889).

Gloria Anzaldúa (1942–2004) was a Texan scholar of Chicana life and cultural, feminist, and queer theory. She made a career out of a variety of freelance teaching, writing, and academic events and is best known for *This Bridge Called My Back: Writings by Radical Women of Color* (1981).

Stephen Aron (b. 1960) is professor of history at the University of California at Los Angeles. His research interests focus on North American frontiers, borderlands, and the American West, as in *American Confluence: The Missouri Frontier from Borderland to Border State* (2009).

George Bancroft (1800–91) was an American historian and politician. His research focused on the history of early America as a product of European settlement and immigration and he is best known for his *History of the United States of America* (10 vols.; 1854–78).

Mark Bassin (b. 1963) is Honorary Senior Research Fellow at the University of Birmingham, UK. He works extensively on the relationship between human societies, politics, and geography.

Charles Beard (1874–1948) was an American historian of America, particularly its social and economic history, and founder of the New History*. He is best known for his reading of the American constitution as an act of economic self-interest, *An Economic Interpretation of the Constitution of the United States* (1913).

Herbert Eugene Bolton (1870–1953) was an American historian who worked on the history of American-Spanish borderlands, a topical subject in view of Spain's colonization of large swathes of South America in the nineteenth century. He was a student of Turner's but disagreed with the frontier thesis because he thought American history could only be understood by looking at all the circumstances of early America, both inside and outside North America.

Edward Channing (1856–1931) was a historian of American history and historiography. Although largely unknown now, he was a leading figure in the formation of the history profession in the USA and wrote major histories of America, such as *A History of the United States* (6 vols., 1905–25).

William "Buffalo Bill" Cody (1846–1917) was a soldier and bison-hunter who founded "Buffalo Bill's Wild West" in 1883, a show based on life in the American West, particularly conflicts between Native Americans and white settlers. The show toured the United States and Europe successfully for over two decades.

William Cronon (b. 1954) is Frederick Jackson Turner and Vilas Research Professor of History, Geography, and Environmental Studies at the University of Wisconsin–Madison. In 2012, he served as President of the American Historical Association, and he is widely regarded as the founder of modern environmental history, including *Nature's Metropolis: Chicago and the Great West* (1991).

John Dewey (1859–1952) was an American psychologist, philosopher, and leading educational reformer, whose work informed Charles Beard* and other founders of the New History.* His works include *How We Think* (1910).

Jared Diamond (b.1937) is an American scientist and author best known for his popular works of science fiction. His Pulitzer prize-winning book, *Guns, Germs, and Steel* (2005), combines knowledge of history, geography, and anthropology to argue that environmental factors, rather than race or culture, explain the dominance of one culture over another.

William Dunning (1857–1922) was an American historian of the British Empire and the American Civil War. His 1907 book, *Reconstruction: Political and Economic*, created the Dunning school, which was influential until the 1930s.

John Mack Faragher (b. 1945) is an American historian of American history. Faragher's work has operated within the field of Western history established by Turner. He has produced a number of works investigating areas neglected by Turner, such as the lives of ordinary individuals, women, and trade, as in *A Great and Noble Scheme: The Tragic Story of the Expulsion of the French Acadians from their American Homeland* (2005).

Lacy K. Ford is an American historian of American history, particularly the South. Ford is currently professor, vice provost, and dean of graduate studies at the University of South Carolina. Among his many prize-winning works is *Origins of Southern Radicalism: The South Carolina Upcountry, 1800–1860* (1988).

Paul Wallace Gates (1901–99) was an American historian of America who is remembered as the leading authority on the history of land policy across the USA. He is best known for *Fifty Million Acres: Conflicts Over Kansas Land Policy, 1854–1890* (1997).

Edward Everett Hale (1822–1909) was an American author, historian, and religious figure. Hale's work with the church brought him into contact with an array of questions on social justice and the nature and characteristics of modern America, topics on which the two magazines he founded promoted awareness (*Old and New*, 1870–5 and *Lend a Hand*, 1886–97).

Albert Bushnell Hart (1854–1943) was an American historian principally of American history. Along with Turner, he campaigned for wide-ranging improvements in historical education, writing books with a similar purpose to Turner, such as *We and Our History* (1923).

Louis Hartz (1919–86) was an American political scientist, best known for his studies on the subject of American exceptionalism, the stream of thought to which Turner contributed. His most famous work is *The Liberal Tradition in America* (1955).

Robert Hine (b. 1921) is Professor Emeritus of History at the University of California, Riverside. He is an American historian working in the tradition of Western History founded by Turner; his most recent book on that subject is *The American West: A New Interpretive History* (2000).

Richard Hofstadter (1916–70) was an American historian and public intellectual, a specialist in the intellectual history of America. He participated in the New History;* *The Age of Reform* (1955) best captures his ideals.

John Franklin Jameson (1859–1937) was an American historian of America who did more than anyone besides Herbert Baxter Adams* to promote the professional and institutional organization of history. Among his most notable works is *The American Revolution Considered as a Social Movement* (1926).

John F. Kennedy (1917–63) was an American politician and 35th President of the United States. Kennedy's presidential campaign drew heavily on the metaphor of the frontier, akin to Turner's.

Patricia Nelson Limerick (b. 1951) is widely considered to be the leading American historian of the American West. She currently holds the posts of Professor of History and chair of the Board of the Center of the American West at the University of Colorado at Boulder. Her reputation has grown since the publication of *The Legacy of Conquest* (1987).

Charles S. Peirce (1839–1914) was an American philosopher and mathematician whose philosophy focused on finding practical solutions to everyday problems.

George W. Pierson (1904–93) was an American historian who occupied the chair of Larned Professor of History at Yale University before retirement. He wrote widely on the origins of modern America in, for example, *The Moving America* (1973).

David Richter (b. 1954) is an American historian of the American West, currently the Roy F. and Jeannette P. Nichols Professor of History at the University of Pennsylvania and Richard S. Dunn Director of the McNeil Center for Early American Studies. He works within a framework set by Turner, exploring how free land fed into American colonization and the formation of American society in *Trade, Land, Power: The Struggle for Eastern North America* (2013).

Theodore Roosevelt (1858–1919) was an American politician, author, and historian who served as 26th President of the United States between 1901 and 1909. Turner encountered Roosevelt personally, as Roosevelt's political career took him to Wisconsin, where he campaigned for social reform and the improvement of ordinary peoples' lives. His work in Wisconsin meant it became known as the "laboratory of democracy."

Arthur Meier Schlesinger Sr. (1888–1965) was an American historian of American history whose work, like that of other contributors to the New History,* focused in particular on social and urban history. *New Viewpoints in American History* (1922) is among his best-known works.

Sacajawea (1788–1812) was a member of a Native American group from the north, known as the Lemhi Shoshone. She assisted Meriwether Lewis and William Clark on their expedition into the Western United States from North Dakota to the Pacific Ocean between 1804 and 1806.

Richard White (b. 1947) is an American historian of the American West who has written widely on the West, Native Americans, and the growth and development of US infrastructure, especially railroads. *Railroaded: The Transcontinentals and the Making of Modern America* (2011) is one of his more recent works.

Willam Appleman Williams (1921–90) was an American historian of American diplomatic history who worked at the University of Wisconsin–Madison. His work critiqued American foreign policy as imperialist, as in *Empire as a Way of Life: An Essay on the Causes and Character of America's Present Predicament, Along With a Few Thoughts About an Alternative* (1980).

Woodrow Wilson (1856–1924) was an American historian and 28th President of the United States. Wilson was a democratic politician and as President had the approval of Turner and New Historians* for keeping America out of World War I for as long as possible, even after the sinking of an American cruise liner, the *Lusitania*, in 1915.

Benjamin Wright (1900–76) was an American political scientist and scholar of American politics and history. *Consensus and Continuity 1776–1787* (1958) is among his central works.

York (1770–1822) was an African American slave now remembered for his participation in Lewis and Clark's journey* as William Clark's slave. He performed extremely hard physical labor during the expedition for no pay.

WORKS CITED

WORKS CITED

Adams, Herbert Baxter. *The German Origin of New England Towns.* Baltimore, MD: Johns Hopkins UP, 1882.

———. and George L. Fox, Albert Bushnell Hart, Charles Homer Haskins, Lucy M. Salmon and H. Morse Stephens. *The Study of History in Schools.* New York: Macmillan, 1899.

Anderson, Benedict R. *Imagined Communities: Reflections on the Origin and Spread of Nationalism.* London: Verso, 1983.

Anzaldúa, Gloria. *Borderlands/La Frontera: The New Mestiza.* 3rd edn. San Francisco: Aunt Lute Books, 2007 (1987).

Aron, Stephen. "Frontiers, Borderlands, Wests." In *American History Now*, edited by Eric Foner and Lisa McGirr, 261–84. Philadelphia: Temple University Press, 2011.

Bancroft, George. *History of the United States from the Discovery of the American Continent.* 6 vols. Boston, MA: Little and Brown, 1834.

Barclay, David E. and Elisabeth Glaser-Schmidt, eds. *Transatlantic Images and Perceptions: Germany and America Since 1776.* Cambridge: Cambridge UP, 1997.

Bassin, Mark. "Turner, Solov'ev, and The 'Frontier Hypothesis': The Nationalist Signification of Open Spaces." *Journal of Modern History* 65, no. 3 (1993): 473–511.

Beard, Charles A., and Mary Ritter Beard. *The Rise of American Civilization.* New York: The Macmillan Company, 1927.

Bender, Thomas, ed. *Rethinking American History in a Global Age.* Berkeley, CA: California UP, 2002.

Bentley, Michael. *Modernizing England's Past: English Historiography in the Age of Modernism 1870–1970.* Cambridge: Cambridge, UP, 2005.

Bestor Jr., Arthur E. "The Transformation of American Scholarship, 1875–1917." *The Library Quarterly* 23, no. 3 (1953): 164–79.

Billington, Ray Allen. *The Genesis of the Frontier Thesis: A Study in Historical Creativity.* San Marino, CA: The Huntington Library, 1971.

———. *Frederick Jackson Turner: Historian, Scholar, Teacher.* Oxford: Oxford UP, 1973.

Boag, Peter. *Re-dressing America's Frontier Past.* Berkeley, CA: California UP, 2011.

Bogue, Allan G. "Frederick Jackson Turner Reconsidered." *History Teacher* 27, no. 2 (1994): 195–221.

—— ——. "'Not by Bread Alone': The Emergence of the Wisconsin Idea and the Departure of Frederick Jackson Turner." *Wisconsin Magazine of History* 86, no. 1 (2002): 10–23.

Bolton, Herbert Eugene. *The Spanish Borderlands: A Chronicle of Old Florida and the Southwest*. Albuquerque: University of New Mexico Press, 1996 (1921).

Breisach, Ernst. *American Progressive History: An Experiment in Modernization*. Chicago, IL: Chicago UP, 1993.

Channing, Edward. *A History of the United States*. 6 vols. New York: Macmillan, 1905–25.

Cronon, William. *Changes in the Land: Indians, Colonists, and the Ecology of New England*. New York: Hill and Wang, 1983.

—— ——. *Nature's Metropolis: Chicago and the Great West*. New York: W.W. Norton, 1991.

—— ——. "Revisiting the Vanishing Frontier: The Legacy of Frederick Jackson Turner." *Western Historical Quarterly* 18, no. 2 (1987): 157–76.

Dewey, John. *Democracy and Education.* New York: Henry Holt, 1914.

Dunning, William A. *The British Empire and the United States: A Review of their Relations During the Century of Peace Following the Treaty of Ghent*. New York: Scribner's Sons, 1914).

Evans, Julie, Ann Genovese, Alexander Reilly and Patrick Wolfe, eds. *Sovereignty: Frontiers of Possibility.* Honolulu, HI: Hawaii UP, 2012.

Faragher, John Mack, ed. *Rereading Frederick Jackson Turner: "The Significance of the Frontier in American History" and Other Essays*. New York: Henry Holt, 1994.

Fling, Fred Morrow. *The Writing of History: An Introduction to Historical Method.* New Haven, CT: Yale UP, 1927.

Ford, Lacy K., Jr. "Frontier Democracy: The Turner Thesis Revisited." *Journal of the Early Republic* 13, no. 2 (1993): 144–63.

Gates, Paul Wallace. *Fifty Million Acres: Conflicts Over Kansas Land Policy, 1854–1890*. New York, NY: Arno Press, 1954.

Grossman, James R., ed. *The Frontier in American Culture: An Exhibition at the Newberry Library, August 26, 1994–January 7, 1995*. Berkeley, CA: California UP, 1994.

Hartz, Louis. *The Liberal Tradition in America: An Interpretation of American Political Thought since the Revolution*. New York: Harcourt, 1955.

Haskell, Thomas L. *The Emergence of Professional Social Science: The American Social Science Association and the Nineteenth-Century Crisis of Authority*. Baltimore, MD: Johns Hopkins UP, 1977.

Higham, John. *History: Professional Scholarship in America*. Baltimore, MD: Johns Hopkins UP, 1983.

Hine, Robert V. and John Mack Faragher. *Frontiers: A Short History of the American West*. New Haven: Yale University Press, 2007.

Hofstadter, Richard. "Turner and the Frontier Myth." *American Scholar* 18, no. 4 (1949): 433–43.

Hughes-Warrington, Marnie. "Frederick Jackson Turner (1861–1932)." In *Fifty Key Thinkers on History*. London: Routledge, 2000.

Hurt, R. Douglas. "Reflections on American Agricultural History." *The Agricultural History Review* 52, no. 1 (2004): 1–19.

Johnson, Benjamin and Andrew R. Graybill, eds. *Bridging National Borders in North America*. Durham, NC: Duke UP, 2010.

Leong, Karen J. "Still Walking, Still Brave: Mapping Gender, Race, and Power in U.S. Western History." *Pacific Historical Review* 79, no. 4 (2010): 618–28.

Limerick, Patricia Nelson. "The Adventures of the Frontier in the Twentieth Century." In *The Frontier in American Culture,* edited by James R. Grossman, 67–102. Berkeley, CA: California UP, 1994.

— — —. *The Legacy of Conquest: The Unbroken Past of the American West.* New York: Norton, 1988.

Lipset, Seymour Martin. *American Exceptionalism: A Double-Edged Sword.* New York: Norton, 1996.

Meany, Edmond S. "Review of Frederick Jackson Turner, *The Frontier in American History*." *The Washington Historical Quarterly* 12, no. 1 (1921): 73.

— — —. "Review of Frederick Jackson Turner, *The Significance of Sections in American History*." *Washington Historical Quarterly* 24, no. 4 (1933): 304.

Nash, Gerald D. *Creating the West: Historical Interpretations 1890–1990.* Albuquerque: University of New Mexico Press, 1991.

Novick, Peter. *That Noble Dream: The "Objectivity" Question and the American Historical Profession*. Cambridge: Cambridge UP, 1988.

Peirce, Charles S. "How to Make Our Ideas Clear." In *Chance, Love and Logic,* edited by Morris R. Cohen. New York: Harcourt Brace, 1923. 55–7.

Pierson, George W. "The Frontier and the Frontiersmen of Turner's Essay." *Pennsylvannia Magazine of History and Biography* 64, no. 4 (1940): 449–78.

Reeves, Thomas C. *Twentieth-Century America: A Brief History.* Oxford: Oxford UP, 2000.

Richter, Daniel K. *Facing East from Indian Country: A Native History of Early America*. Cambridge, MA: Harvard University Press, 2001.

Ridge, Martin. "The Life of an Idea: The Significance of Frederick Jackson Turner's Frontier Thesis." *The Magazine of Western History* 41, no. 1 (1991): 2–13.

— — —. "Turner the Historian: A Long Shadow." *Journal of the Early Republic* 13, no. 2 (1993): 133–44.

Riley, Glenda. "Frederick Jackson Turner Overlooked the Ladies." *Journal of the Early Republic* 13, no. 2 (1993): 216–30.

Ringer, Fritz K. *The Decline of the Mandarins: The German Academic Community, 1890–1933.* Cambridge, MA: Harvard UP, 1969.

Rodgers, Daniel T. *Age of Fracture*. Cambridge, MA: Harvard UP, 2011.

———. "Exceptionalism." In *Imagined Histories: American Historians Interpret the Past*, edited by Gordon Wood and Anthony Molho, 24–36. Princeton, NJ: Princeton UP, 1998.

Santos, Fernanda. "Arizona: Most of Law on Ethnic Studies is Upheld." *New York Times,* March 11, 2013. Accessed March 1, 2015. http://www.nytimes.com/2013/03/12/education/most-of-arizona-law-on-ethnic-studies-is-upheld.html?_r=0.

Steiner, Michael. "From Frontier to Region: Frederick Jackson Turner and the New Western History." *Pacific Historical Review* 64, no. 4 (1995): 479–501.

Tendler, Joseph. *Opponents of the Annales School.* Basingstoke: Palgrave, 2013.

Tindall, George Brown and Shi, David Emory, *America: A Narrative History*. New York: Norton, 2007.

Turner, Frederick Jackson. *The Character and Influence of the Fur Trade in Wisconsin*. Cambridge, MA: Harvard UP, 1889.

———. "The Significance of the Frontier in American History." In *The Frontier in American History*. New York, NY: Henry Holt, 1921, 1–38.

———. *The Significance of Sections in American History*, edited by Max Farrand. New York, NY: Henry Holt, 1932.

———. . "Social Forces in American History." *American Historical Review* 16, no. 2 (1911): 217–33.

Tyler, Daniel, ed. *Western American History in the Seventies: Selected Papers Presented to the First Western History Conference, Colorado State University, August 10–12, 1972.* Fort Collins, CO: Robinson for Educational Media & Information Systems, 1972.

Uekoetter, Frank, ed. *The Turning Points of Environmental History*. Pittsburgh, PA: Pittsburgh UP, 2010.

White, Richard. *The Middle Ground: Indians, Empires, and Republics in the Great Lakes Region, 1650–1815.* New York: Cambridge University Press, 1991.

———*"It's Your Misfortune and None of My Own": A History of the American West*. Norman, OK: Oklahoma UP, 1991.

Widder, Keith R. *Beyond Pontiac's Shadow: Michilimackinac and the Anglo-Indian War of 1763.* East Lansing, MI: Michigan State University Press, 2013.

Wood, Gordon and Anthony Molho, eds. *Imagined Histories: American Historians Interpret the Past.* Princeton, NJ: Princeton UP, 1998.

THE MACAT LIBRARY
BY DISCIPLINE

AFRICANA STUDIES

Chinua Achebe's *An Image of Africa: Racism in Conrad's Heart of Darkness*
W. E. B. Du Bois's *The Souls of Black Folk*
Zora Neale Huston's *Characteristics of Negro Expression*
Martin Luther King Jr's *Why We Can't Wait*
Toni Morrison's *Playing in the Dark: Whiteness in the American Literary Imagination*

ANTHROPOLOGY

Arjun Appadurai's *Modernity at Large: Cultural Dimensions of Globalisation*
Philippe Ariès's *Centuries of Childhood*
Franz Boas's *Race, Language and Culture*
Kim Chan & Renée Mauborgne's *Blue Ocean Strategy*
Jared Diamond's *Guns, Germs & Steel: the Fate of Human Societies*
Jared Diamond's *Collapse: How Societies Choose to Fail or Survive*
E. E. Evans-Pritchard's *Witchcraft, Oracles and Magic Among the Azande*
James Ferguson's *The Anti-Politics Machine*
Clifford Geertz's *The Interpretation of Cultures*
David Graeber's *Debt: the First 5000 Years*
Karen Ho's *Liquidated: An Ethnography of Wall Street*
Geert Hofstede's *Culture's Consequences: Comparing Values, Behaviors, Institutes and Organizations across Nations*
Claude Lévi-Strauss's *Structural Anthropology*
Jay Macleod's *Ain't No Makin' It: Aspirations and Attainment in a Low-Income Neighborhood*
Saba Mahmood's *The Politics of Piety: The Islamic Revival and the Feminist Subject*
Marcel Mauss's *The Gift*

BUSINESS

Jean Lave & Etienne Wenger's *Situated Learning*
Theodore Levitt's *Marketing Myopia*
Burton G. Malkiel's *A Random Walk Down Wall Street*
Douglas McGregor's *The Human Side of Enterprise*
Michael Porter's *Competitive Strategy: Creating and Sustaining Superior Performance*
John Kotter's *Leading Change*
C. K. Prahalad & Gary Hamel's *The Core Competence of the Corporation*

CRIMINOLOGY

Michelle Alexander's *The New Jim Crow: Mass Incarceration in the Age of Colorblindness*
Michael R. Gottfredson & Travis Hirschi's *A General Theory of Crime*
Richard Herrnstein & Charles A. Murray's *The Bell Curve: Intelligence and Class Structure in American Life*
Elizabeth Loftus's *Eyewitness Testimony*
Jay Macleod's *Ain't No Makin' It: Aspirations and Attainment in a Low-Income Neighborhood*
Philip Zimbardo's *The Lucifer Effect*

ECONOMICS

Janet Abu-Lughod's *Before European Hegemony*
Ha-Joon Chang's *Kicking Away the Ladder*
David Brion Davis's *The Problem of Slavery in the Age of Revolution*
Milton Friedman's *The Role of Monetary Policy*
Milton Friedman's *Capitalism and Freedom*
David Graeber's *Debt: the First 5000 Years*
Friedrich Hayek's *The Road to Serfdom*
Karen Ho's *Liquidated: An Ethnography of Wall Street*

John Maynard Keynes's *The General Theory of Employment, Interest and Money*
Charles P. Kindleberger's *Manias, Panics and Crashes*
Robert Lucas's *Why Doesn't Capital Flow from Rich to Poor Countries?*
Burton G. Malkiel's *A Random Walk Down Wall Street*
Thomas Robert Malthus's *An Essay on the Principle of Population*
Karl Marx's *Capital*
Thomas Piketty's *Capital in the Twenty-First Century*
Amartya Sen's *Development as Freedom*
Adam Smith's *The Wealth of Nations*
Nassim Nicholas Taleb's *The Black Swan: The Impact of the Highly Improbable*
Amos Tversky's & Daniel Kahneman's *Judgment under Uncertainty: Heuristics and Biases*
Mahbub Ul Haq's *Reflections on Human Development*
Max Weber's *The Protestant Ethic and the Spirit of Capitalism*

FEMINISM AND GENDER STUDIES

Judith Butler's *Gender Trouble*
Simone De Beauvoir's *The Second Sex*
Michel Foucault's *History of Sexuality*
Betty Friedan's *The Feminine Mystique*
Saba Mahmood's *The Politics of Piety: The Islamic Revival and the Feminist Subject*
Joan Wallach Scott's *Gender and the Politics of History*
Mary Wollstonecraft's *A Vindication of the Rights of Woman*
Virginia Woolf's *A Room of One's Own*

GEOGRAPHY

The Brundtland Report's *Our Common Future*
Rachel Carson's *Silent Spring*
Charles Darwin's *On the Origin of Species*
James Ferguson's *The Anti-Politics Machine*
Jane Jacobs's *The Death and Life of Great American Cities*
James Lovelock's *Gaia: A New Look at Life on Earth*
Amartya Sen's *Development as Freedom*
Mathis Wackernagel & William Rees's *Our Ecological Footprint*

HISTORY

Janet Abu-Lughod's *Before European Hegemony*
Benedict Anderson's *Imagined Communities*
Bernard Bailyn's *The Ideological Origins of the American Revolution*
Hanna Batatu's *The Old Social Classes And The Revolutionary Movements Of Iraq*
Christopher Browning's *Ordinary Men: Reserve Police Batallion 101 and the Final Solution in Poland*
Edmund Burke's *Reflections on the Revolution in France*
William Cronon's *Nature's Metropolis: Chicago And The Great West*
Alfred W. Crosby's *The Columbian Exchange*
Hamid Dabashi's *Iran: A People Interrupted*
David Brion Davis's *The Problem of Slavery in the Age of Revolution*
Nathalie Zemon Davis's *The Return of Martin Guerre*
Jared Diamond's *Guns, Germs & Steel: the Fate of Human Societies*
Frank Dikotter's *Mao's Great Famine*
John W Dower's *War Without Mercy: Race And Power In The Pacific War*
W. E. B. Du Bois's *The Souls of Black Folk*
Richard J. Evans's *In Defence of History*
Lucien Febvre's *The Problem of Unbelief in the 16th Century*
Sheila Fitzpatrick's *Everyday Stalinism*

The Macat Library By Discipline

Eric Foner's *Reconstruction: America's Unfinished Revolution, 1863-1877*
Michel Foucault's *Discipline and Punish*
Michel Foucault's *History of Sexuality*
Francis Fukuyama's *The End of History and the Last Man*
John Lewis Gaddis's *We Now Know: Rethinking Cold War History*
Ernest Gellner's *Nations and Nationalism*
Eugene Genovese's *Roll, Jordan, Roll: The World the Slaves Made*
Carlo Ginzburg's *The Night Battles*
Daniel Goldhagen's *Hitler's Willing Executioners*
Jack Goldstone's *Revolution and Rebellion in the Early Modern World*
Antonio Gramsci's *The Prison Notebooks*
Alexander Hamilton, John Jay & James Madison's *The Federalist Papers*
Christopher Hill's *The World Turned Upside Down*
Carole Hillenbrand's *The Crusades: Islamic Perspectives*
Thomas Hobbes's *Leviathan*
Eric Hobsbawm's *The Age Of Revolution*
John A. Hobson's *Imperialism: A Study*
Albert Hourani's *History of the Arab Peoples*
Samuel P. Huntington's *The Clash of Civilizations and the Remaking of World Order*
C. L. R. James's *The Black Jacobins*
Tony Judt's *Postwar: A History of Europe Since 1945*
Ernst Kantorowicz's *The King's Two Bodies: A Study in Medieval Political Theology*
Paul Kennedy's *The Rise and Fall of the Great Powers*
Ian Kershaw's *The "Hitler Myth": Image and Reality in the Third Reich*
John Maynard Keynes's *The General Theory of Employment, Interest and Money*
Charles P. Kindleberger's *Manias, Panics and Crashes*
Martin Luther King Jr's *Why We Can't Wait*
Henry Kissinger's *World Order: Reflections on the Character of Nations and the Course of History*
Thomas Kuhn's *The Structure of Scientific Revolutions*
Georges Lefebvre's *The Coming of the French Revolution*
John Locke's *Two Treatises of Government*
Niccolò Machiavelli's *The Prince*
Thomas Robert Malthus's *An Essay on the Principle of Population*
Mahmood Mamdani's *Citizen and Subject: Contemporary Africa And The Legacy Of Late Colonialism*
Karl Marx's *Capital*
Stanley Milgram's *Obedience to Authority*
John Stuart Mill's *On Liberty*
Thomas Paine's *Common Sense*
Thomas Paine's *Rights of Man*
Geoffrey Parker's *Global Crisis: War, Climate Change and Catastrophe in the Seventeenth Century*
Jonathan Riley-Smith's *The First Crusade and the Idea of Crusading*
Jean-Jacques Rousseau's *The Social Contract*
Joan Wallach Scott's *Gender and the Politics of History*
Theda Skocpol's *States and Social Revolutions*
Adam Smith's *The Wealth of Nations*
Timothy Snyder's *Bloodlands: Europe Between Hitler and Stalin*
Sun Tzu's *The Art of War*
Keith Thomas's *Religion and the Decline of Magic*
Thucydides's *The History of the Peloponnesian War*
Frederick Jackson Turner's *The Significance of the Frontier in American History*
Odd Arne Westad's *The Global Cold War: Third World Interventions And The Making Of Our Times*

LITERATURE

Chinua Achebe's *An Image of Africa: Racism in Conrad's Heart of Darkness*
Roland Barthes's *Mythologies*
Homi K. Bhabha's *The Location of Culture*
Judith Butler's *Gender Trouble*
Simone De Beauvoir's *The Second Sex*
Ferdinand De Saussure's *Course in General Linguistics*
T. S. Eliot's *The Sacred Wood: Essays on Poetry and Criticism*
Zora Neale Huston's *Characteristics of Negro Expression*
Toni Morrison's *Playing in the Dark: Whiteness in the American Literary Imagination*
Edward Said's *Orientalism*
Gayatri Chakravorty Spivak's *Can the Subaltern Speak?*
Mary Wollstonecraft's *A Vindication of the Rights of Women*
Virginia Woolf's *A Room of One's Own*

PHILOSOPHY

Elizabeth Anscombe's *Modern Moral Philosophy*
Hannah Arendt's *The Human Condition*
Aristotle's *Metaphysics*
Aristotle's *Nicomachean Ethics*
Edmund Gettier's *Is Justified True Belief Knowledge?*
Georg Wilhelm Friedrich Hegel's *Phenomenology of Spirit*
David Hume's *Dialogues Concerning Natural Religion*
David Hume's *The Enquiry for Human Understanding*
Immanuel Kant's *Religion within the Boundaries of Mere Reason*
Immanuel Kant's *Critique of Pure Reason*
Søren Kierkegaard's *The Sickness Unto Death*
Søren Kierkegaard's *Fear and Trembling*
C. S. Lewis's *The Abolition of Man*
Alasdair MacIntyre's *After Virtue*
Marcus Aurelius's *Meditations*
Friedrich Nietzsche's *On the Genealogy of Morality*
Friedrich Nietzsche's *Beyond Good and Evil*
Plato's *Republic*
Plato's *Symposium*
Jean-Jacques Rousseau's *The Social Contract*
Gilbert Ryle's *The Concept of Mind*
Baruch Spinoza's *Ethics*
Sun Tzu's *The Art of War*
Ludwig Wittgenstein's *Philosophical Investigations*

POLITICS

Benedict Anderson's *Imagined Communities*
Aristotle's *Politics*
Bernard Bailyn's *The Ideological Origins of the American Revolution*
Edmund Burke's *Reflections on the Revolution in France*
John C. Calhoun's *A Disquisition on Government*
Ha-Joon Chang's *Kicking Away the Ladder*
Hamid Dabashi's *Iran: A People Interrupted*
Hamid Dabashi's *Theology of Discontent: The Ideological Foundation of the Islamic Revolution in Iran*
Robert Dahl's *Democracy and its Critics*
Robert Dahl's *Who Governs?*
David Brion Davis's *The Problem of Slavery in the Age of Revolution*

The Macat Library By Discipline

Alexis De Tocqueville's *Democracy in America*
James Ferguson's *The Anti-Politics Machine*
Frank Dikotter's *Mao's Great Famine*
Sheila Fitzpatrick's *Everyday Stalinism*
Eric Foner's *Reconstruction: America's Unfinished Revolution, 1863-1877*
Milton Friedman's *Capitalism and Freedom*
Francis Fukuyama's *The End of History and the Last Man*
John Lewis Gaddis's *We Now Know: Rethinking Cold War History*
Ernest Gellner's *Nations and Nationalism*
David Graeber's *Debt: the First 5000 Years*
Antonio Gramsci's *The Prison Notebooks*
Alexander Hamilton, John Jay & James Madison's *The Federalist Papers*
Friedrich Hayek's *The Road to Serfdom*
Christopher Hill's *The World Turned Upside Down*
Thomas Hobbes's *Leviathan*
John A. Hobson's *Imperialism: A Study*
Samuel P. Huntington's *The Clash of Civilizations and the Remaking of World Order*
Tony Judt's *Postwar: A History of Europe Since 1945*
David C. Kang's *China Rising: Peace, Power and Order in East Asia*
Paul Kennedy's *The Rise and Fall of Great Powers*
Robert Keohane's *After Hegemony*
Martin Luther King Jr.'s *Why We Can't Wait*
Henry Kissinger's *World Order: Reflections on the Character of Nations and the Course of History*
John Locke's *Two Treatises of Government*
Niccolò Machiavelli's *The Prince*
Thomas Robert Malthus's *An Essay on the Principle of Population*
Mahmood Mamdani's *Citizen and Subject: Contemporary Africa And The Legacy Of Late Colonialism*
Karl Marx's *Capital*
John Stuart Mill's *On Liberty*
John Stuart Mill's *Utilitarianism*
Hans Morgenthau's *Politics Among Nations*
Thomas Paine's *Common Sense*
Thomas Paine's *Rights of Man*
Thomas Piketty's *Capital in the Twenty-First Century*
Robert D. Putman's *Bowling Alone*
John Rawls's *Theory of Justice*
Jean-Jacques Rousseau's *The Social Contract*
Theda Skocpol's *States and Social Revolutions*
Adam Smith's *The Wealth of Nations*
Sun Tzu's *The Art of War*
Henry David Thoreau's *Civil Disobedience*
Thucydides's *The History of the Peloponnesian War*
Kenneth Waltz's *Theory of International Politics*
Max Weber's *Politics as a Vocation*
Odd Arne Westad's *The Global Cold War: Third World Interventions And The Making Of Our Times*

POSTCOLONIAL STUDIES

Roland Barthes's *Mythologies*
Frantz Fanon's *Black Skin, White Masks*
Homi K. Bhabha's *The Location of Culture*
Gustavo Gutiérrez's *A Theology of Liberation*
Edward Said's *Orientalism*
Gayatri Chakravorty Spivak's *Can the Subaltern Speak?*

PSYCHOLOGY

Gordon Allport's *The Nature of Prejudice*
Alan Baddeley & Graham Hitch's *Aggression: A Social Learning Analysis*
Albert Bandura's *Aggression: A Social Learning Analysis*
Leon Festinger's *A Theory of Cognitive Dissonance*
Sigmund Freud's *The Interpretation of Dreams*
Betty Friedan's *The Feminine Mystique*
Michael R. Gottfredson & Travis Hirschi's *A General Theory of Crime*
Eric Hoffer's *The True Believer: Thoughts on the Nature of Mass Movements*
William James's *Principles of Psychology*
Elizabeth Loftus's *Eyewitness Testimony*
A. H. Maslow's *A Theory of Human Motivation*
Stanley Milgram's *Obedience to Authority*
Steven Pinker's *The Better Angels of Our Nature*
Oliver Sacks's *The Man Who Mistook His Wife For a Hat*
Richard Thaler & Cass Sunstein's *Nudge: Improving Decisions About Health, Wealth and Happiness*
Amos Tversky's *Judgment under Uncertainty: Heuristics and Biases*
Philip Zimbardo's *The Lucifer Effect*

SCIENCE

Rachel Carson's *Silent Spring*
William Cronon's *Nature's Metropolis: Chicago And The Great West*
Alfred W. Crosby's *The Columbian Exchange*
Charles Darwin's *On the Origin of Species*
Richard Dawkin's *The Selfish Gene*
Thomas Kuhn's *The Structure of Scientific Revolutions*
Geoffrey Parker's *Global Crisis: War, Climate Change and Catastrophe in the Seventeenth Century*
Mathis Wackernagel & William Rees's *Our Ecological Footprint*

SOCIOLOGY

Michelle Alexander's *The New Jim Crow: Mass Incarceration in the Age of Colorblindness*
Gordon Allport's *The Nature of Prejudice*
Albert Bandura's *Aggression: A Social Learning Analysis*
Hanna Batatu's *The Old Social Classes And The Revolutionary Movements Of Iraq*
Ha-Joon Chang's *Kicking Away the Ladder*
W. E. B. Du Bois's *The Souls of Black Folk*
Émile Durkheim's *On Suicide*
Frantz Fanon's *Black Skin, White Masks*
Frantz Fanon's *The Wretched of the Earth*
Eric Foner's *Reconstruction: America's Unfinished Revolution, 1863-1877*
Eugene Genovese's *Roll, Jordan, Roll: The World the Slaves Made*
Jack Goldstone's *Revolution and Rebellion in the Early Modern World*
Antonio Gramsci's *The Prison Notebooks*
Richard Herrnstein & Charles A Murray's *The Bell Curve: Intelligence and Class Structure in American Life*
Eric Hoffer's *The True Believer: Thoughts on the Nature of Mass Movements*
Jane Jacobs's *The Death and Life of Great American Cities*
Robert Lucas's *Why Doesn't Capital Flow from Rich to Poor Countries?*
Jay Macleod's *Ain't No Makin' It: Aspirations and Attainment in a Low Income Neighborhood*
Elaine May's *Homeward Bound: American Families in the Cold War Era*
Douglas McGregor's *The Human Side of Enterprise*
C. Wright Mills's *The Sociological Imagination*

The Macat Library By Discipline

Thomas Piketty's *Capital in the Twenty-First Century*
Robert D. Putman's *Bowling Alone*
David Riesman's *The Lonely Crowd: A Study of the Changing American Character*
Edward Said's *Orientalism*
Joan Wallach Scott's *Gender and the Politics of History*
Theda Skocpol's *States and Social Revolutions*
Max Weber's *The Protestant Ethic and the Spirit of Capitalism*

THEOLOGY

Augustine's *Confessions*
Benedict's *Rule of St Benedict*
Gustavo Gutiérrez's *A Theology of Liberation*
Carole Hillenbrand's *The Crusades: Islamic Perspectives*
David Hume's *Dialogues Concerning Natural Religion*
Immanuel Kant's *Religion within the Boundaries of Mere Reason*
Ernst Kantorowicz's *The King's Two Bodies: A Study in Medieval Political Theology*
Søren Kierkegaard's *The Sickness Unto Death*
C. S. Lewis's *The Abolition of Man*
Saba Mahmood's *The Politics of Piety: The Islamic Revival and the Feminist Subjec*t
Baruch Spinoza's *Ethics*
Keith Thomas's *Religion and the Decline of Magic*

COMING SOON

Chris Argyris's *The Individual and the Organisation*
Seyla Benhabib's *The Rights of Others*
Walter Benjamin's *The Work Of Art in the Age of Mechanical Reproduction*
John Berger's *Ways of Seeing*
Pierre Bourdieu's *Outline of a Theory of Practice*
Mary Douglas's *Purity and Danger*
Roland Dworkin's *Taking Rights Seriously*
James G. March's *Exploration and Exploitation in Organisational Learning*
Ikujiro Nonaka's *A Dynamic Theory of Organizational Knowledge Creation*
Griselda Pollock's *Vision and Difference*
Amartya Sen's *Inequality Re-Examined*
Susan Sontag's *On Photography*
Yasser Tabbaa's *The Transformation of Islamic Art*
Ludwig von Mises's *Theory of Money and Credit*

Macat Disciplines

Access the greatest ideas and thinkers across entire disciplines, including

INEQUALITY

Ha-Joon Chang's, *Kicking Away the Ladder*

David Graeber's, *Debt: The First 5000 Years*

Robert E. Lucas's, *Why Doesn't Capital Flow from Rich To Poor Countries?*

Thomas Piketty's, *Capital in the Twenty-First Century*

Amartya Sen's, *Inequality Re-Examined*

Mahbub Ul Haq's, *Reflections on Human Development*

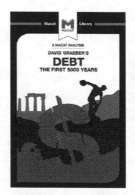

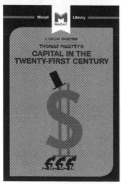

Macat analyses are available from all good bookshops and libraries.

Access hundreds of analyses through one, multimedia tool.
Join free for one month **library.macat.com**

Macat Disciplines

Access the greatest ideas and thinkers across entire disciplines, including

GLOBALIZATION

Arjun Appadurai's, *Modernity at Large: Cultural Dimensions of Globalisation*

James Ferguson's, *The Anti-Politics Machine*

Geert Hofstede's, *Culture's Consequences*

Amartya Sen's, *Development as Freedom*

Macat Disciplines

Access the greatest ideas and thinkers across entire disciplines, including

THE FUTURE OF DEMOCRACY

Robert A. Dahl's, *Democracy and Its Critics*
Robert A. Dahl's, *Who Governs?*
Alexis De Toqueville's, *Democracy in America*
Niccolò Machiavelli's, *The Prince*
John Stuart Mill's, *On Liberty*
Robert D. Putnam's, *Bowling Alone*
Jean-Jacques Rousseau's, *The Social Contract*
Henry David Thoreau's, *Civil Disobedience*

Macat analyses are available from all good bookshops and libraries.

Access hundreds of analyses through one, multimedia tool.
Join free for one month **library.macat.com**

Macat Disciplines

Access the greatest ideas and thinkers across entire disciplines, including

TOTALITARIANISM

Sheila Fitzpatrick's, *Everyday Stalinism*
Ian Kershaw's, *The "Hitler Myth"*
Timothy Snyder's, *Bloodlands*

Macat Pairs

*Analyse historical and modern issues
from opposite sides of an argument.
Pairs include:*

Printed in the United States
by Baker & Taylor Publisher Services